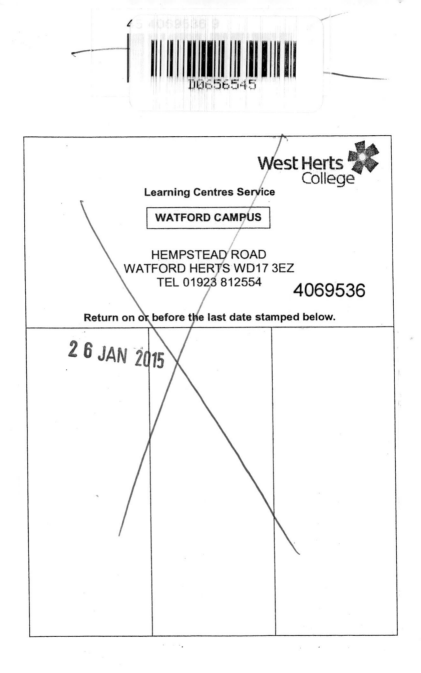

West Herts College

Learning Centres Service

WATFORD CAMPUS

HEMPSTEAD ROAD
WATFORD HERTS WD17 3EZ
TEL 01923 812554

4069536

Return on or before the last date stamped below.

2 6 JAN 2015

WATFORD LRC

Performing Live Comedy

CHRIS RITCHIE

Methuen Drama

Published by Methuen Drama 2012

Methuen Drama, an imprint of Bloomsbury Publishing Plc
1 3 5 7 9 10 8 6 4 2
Methuen Drama
Bloomsbury Publishing Plc
50 Bedford Square
London WC1B 3DP
www.methuendrama.com

A CIP catalogue record for this book is available from the British Library

ISBN: 978 1 408 14643 9

Available in the USA from Bloomsbury Academic & Professional, 175 Fifth Avenue/3rd Floor, New York, NY 10010

Typeset by MATS Typesetters, Leigh-on-Sea, Essex

Printed and bound in India by Replika Press Pvt. Ltd.

Caution

Contents

Acknowledgements

Thank you to all the comedians and others mentioned in here who kindly lent me their time and wisdom. Mucho obligado! Thank you also to Anna Brewer at Methuen Drama for her patience and insights, and to Michael Harrington for his hard work and care over the design. But, most of all, thank you, H, for reading the manuscript, giving so much constructive criticism and doing the drawings. Your incredible tolerance is very much appreciated. This book is dedicated to all my students, past and present, on the comedy degree at Solent. You have taught me more than you will ever know.

Introduction

Comedy is a global, multi-billion dollar industry, which includes film, TV, theatre, DVDs, radio and live performance. Performing live is probably the easiest way to start a career in comedy. In other areas – film, music, theatre – there are logistical problems that often seem insurmountable: the making and, most of all, the distribution of a film; finding other musicians who you can stand to be in a band with; organising a cast and rehearsal space for a play, and so on. Performing live comedy merely needs a room, a small audience and the bottle to get up there and do it. Oh, and jokes.

Given enough aptitude for comedy, it is a craft that can be learned in the same way as film making, music or acting. If something can be explained and repeated, then it can be taught. Some comedians fear that their 'comedy magic' will disappear if they scrutinise it too much. Others feel that being taught about comedy cannot make you a better comedian. This is as ridiculous as saying that the less architects know about architecture, the better their buildings will be.

Comedians come from all sorts of different backgrounds. Many start doing live comedy because someone has said, 'You should be on the stage' (to which the European Union standard punchline #1429 is 'Yeah, the next stage out of town'). And indeed this is a good indication that you can tell a story, hold attention and entertain people. However, being funny in the pub and being funny onstage are different. Onstage, you are expected to present a coherent character or persona, with an organised set, or routine, that develops as it goes along while providing a laugh every minute or so.

This book is for all those playground and pub comedians who are ready to take the next step. It is aimed at people who have always wanted to try performing live comedy and those who are obsessed with comedy and find that being funny is a creative outlet for their personalities.

The students in the comedy degree course I started at Southampton Solent University are a diverse lot, but most of them share an irrepressible enthusiasm for comedy as a way of self-expression. They are the ones who watch and re-watch endless DVDs (including the extras), are at the front of the queues for tickets to see the latest show in town, and recognise the infinite possibilities of comedy. And it is to them that this book is dedicated.

This book looks at all aspects of performing live comedy: from how to write material to structuring a stage persona, from organising an open-mic spot to running your own venue. It is aimed at comedians who are just about to start their careers as well as those who have got a few gigs under their belts.

The comedians

The book starts with a look at the top comedians of today and yesterday, who have had a major impact on comedy.

The language

In comedy there are specialised words and phrases that everyone uses, so I have included a comprehensive list at the start, which will save a lot of explaining as the book goes on.

Comedy

A lot of things have changed in the 2,500 years that live comedy has been around but some things remain the same. Comedians have always made jokes about toilets, bottoms, sex and politics and always will. Taboos and controversies change over time: what was okay to say on the live comedy stage once may not be acceptable today. And what is not acceptable one day can be a major theme for comedians the next. Comedy reflects the world and all the people in it, and they are constantly evolving.

The performer

The identity of a performer is every bit as important as what they say because the audience builds a relationship with them while they are onstage. We can draw on physical aspects of ourselves and communicate our way of looking at the world or we can develop a comic character that allows us to talk about things from a different perspective. People tend to think of live comedy as a bloke onstage with a microphone, but this book also looks at other possibilities such as duos, ventriloquists, music and character acts. In addition, it examines how sexuality, gender, ethnicity and even, in some cases, disability can be used to create a comic identity. If you want to know about comedy, ask a comedian, so I asked for and got some valuable advice from comedians and writers currently on the circuit on how to use different skills and techniques in order to get laughs. This advice is threaded throughout the book.

The comic character and others

Comic characters can be very useful for performing material that we may not be able to do as 'ourselves', and the book takes a look at diverse examples such as Dame Edna Everage, Neil Hamburger and Al Murray's Pub Landlord. These characters are satirical, or use controversial and outrageous comedy that a 'real person' may not get away with.

The performance

Every performance is different, but they all follow the same basic rules. In this chapter we look at the whole process, from how we introduce ourselves to how we say thank you and get offstage, as well as how to deal with the microphone and other stage techniques. How to get gigs and what kind of gigs to look out for are included here, along with the vital importance of self-confidence, self-discipline and adequate preparation.

Jokes

The vehicle of comedy is jokes, and this chapter looks at everything from writing the simplest gag to developing it into a professional routine. There are plenty of exercises to get you working on different kinds of material. We also explore satire and topicality, taboos and rudeness! Knowing what not to joke about is as important as what you *can* joke about, so a short lesson in ethics is involved.

The audience

Many comedians see the audience as something to conquer, a beast to vanquish; in fact, comedy language is full of assault, killing and dying. The audience-performer relationship can seem quite adversarial in the hands of some comedians, but it can be a positive element: any audience is a wonderfully bizarre and unique thing, to be enjoyed as well as respected. This chapter looks at the different audiences and the expectations they bring to the show. It also demystifies the dreaded heckler. Many experienced comedians have devised techniques for making hecklers less of a threat and even using them to enhance a performance. We show you how to prepare for the worst as well as the best kind of heckler, so as not to miss any comic opportunities.

The comedy industry

Comedy is big business and can be lucrative for a performer; and we need to know the basics of how it works. Of course, nothing is better than experience, but if we listen to the advice of professionals we can avoid some of the more unpleasant pitfalls of building a career in performing live comedy. We look at simple things such as stage names and publicity photos, as well as giving tips on how to be professional and market oneself through an Internet presence.

We also look at comedy around the world. Now that we live in an age of cheap travel, visiting another country means we can perform there also. Live comedy is not restricted to English-speaking countries: there is a growing European circuit, which can be accessed with a bit of local knowledge. Besides talking to British and American comedians, we talk to people in Australia, Germany and Israel about what they do there and how we can perform in these places. The organisers of these events give valuable advice here.

If there is nowhere in your neighbourhood to perform, it is not difficult to organise an open-mic night at a convenient and suitable venue. Enthusiasm, rudimentary sound equipment and a half-decent spotlight can transform an ordinary space into an intimate and successful comedy venue. Running a comedy night can be a fascinating challenge. The few simple rules to follow are outlined here by people experienced in running them. Via the Internet, you can contact other comedians in the vicinity and engage them to perform there. Where there is a space for comedy, comedians will find it.

Performing Live Comedy uses well-known examples from the last thirty years of comedy that any comedy fan will know about which are available on DVD or can be found on YouTube (an invaluable comedy resource). The book is full of practical advice from established comedians on the current circuit who come from different backgrounds, men and women, both disabled and able-bodied. As well as comedians, this book also draws on the advice of other more 'backstage operators' – writers, journalists, teachers, venue organisers and agents have all been interviewed.

The only thing stopping you is you. (It is assumed you are interested, otherwise you would not have read this far. Either that, or someone has bought you the wrong Christmas present. Again.) After reading and heeding the advice in this book, the novice comedian – you – simply needs to pick up the phone (if perhaps with some trepidation) to book your first open-mic spot at the local comedy club. Then your career has started.

1. The Comedians

The following is a top-ten guide to some of the best-known comedians, of today and yesterday, mentioned in this book – artists that any budding comedian or comedy writer should check out. The idea of rating such a subjective thing as comedy is difficult – nigh-on impossible – but this list is based not on how funny a comedian is but on how much they have changed either the form or the content of comedy, or both. It may not include your favourite performer, but it does include people whose unique influence on contemporary comedy has set them apart.

Lenny Bruce Often cited as the first 'alternative comedian', Lenny Bruce actually followed a trend started by Mort Sahl. Lenny did wear the suit (bespoke Italian-style) but his material and his use of language were much more extreme than Sahl's, and he was arrested onstage several times for 'offensive' language. 'Dirty Lenny' pushed the boundaries of what comedians talk about and what language they use in doing it. His highly satirical material dealt with drugs, politics and racism and adopted an anti-establishment approach. He was also a gifted mimic. His 'autobiography', *How to Talk Dirty and Influence People*, is well worth a read, and the biography by Albert Goldman, *Ladies and Gentlemen, Lenny Bruce*, is a fascinating exploration of his life.

Billy Connolly Connolly started off playing banjo in Scottish folk clubs; then gradually his between-song monologues took over his act. However, in the 1970s there were few comedy venues that welcomed material dealing with religion, politics, class and sex, and Connolly found his audience instead in the rock world, most unusually supporting Elton John on a tour of the United States in 1976. As British alternative comedy developed in the 1980s, more theatres, clubs and gig venues began to offer stand-up, and Connolly became the most successful comedian of his generation. His thick Glaswegian accent, scruffy appearance and foul-mouthed though genial comedy made a hit with punters, and Connolly came to occupy a place in UK comedy that the likes of Mort Sahl and Lenny Bruce had claimed in the States. His fast and iconoclastic comedy, peppered with swear words, has remained an inspiration to a new generation of comedians while continuing to delight comedy fans.

Tommy Cooper As the self-styled 'anti-comedian' Ed Aczel once said, 'The Tommy Cooper approach is "This is disastrous but nevertheless it is the show".' Cooper presented a shambolic comic/magician whose tricks and gags often failed, thus making the successful ones seem all the better. Of course, it was all planned. With his large frame, tatty fez and 'just like that' catchphrase, Tommy was ahead of his time, a true original and a maverick. Despite his heavy drinking and unpleasant offstage personality, Cooper onstage had a kind of charm. He was instantly recognisable and was one of the first comedians to make a success out of 'failure'. Many magicians, prop comics and comedians acknowledge his influence and many appreciate his universal appeal to everyone from children to OAPs.

Les Dawson To judge comedians from previous decades by contemporary standards is often futile, but Les Dawson suffered from this until quite recently. His onstage material focused heavily on jokes about his mother-in-law and his wife, which now seem outdated. However, his misanthropic stage persona and fantastic vocabulary set him apart from the standard variety comedian of the time. Dawson's grotesque world view was simultaneously poetic and grim, framed in an industrial Northern context, but his attitude and imagination were far apart from those of his contemporaries. Like Max Miller, he had only to appear on stage to get the initial laughs he required to get going.

Bill Hicks Today's comedy would not be the same without the influence of Bill Hicks. His free-ranging material covered politics, ethics, drugs, religion, smoking and sex and was fired by a righteous anger at the state of the world in general and his own country, the United States, in particular. He wanted comedy that made people think – 'Chomsky[1] with dick jokes', as he said. He was uncompromising in terms of his material, which deprived him of the TV coverage that many other, lesser comedians received by doing weaker versions of Hicks. However, with his untimely death at the age of thirty-two, his reputation – that of a true comedy legend equal to the rock heroes he often mentioned – was sealed.

Max Miller Once dubbed 'the pure gold of the music hall', Max was at his peak in Britain in the 1940s. He constantly challenged what comedians were – or, rather, were not – allowed to discuss. Although his material now seems dated and often obscure, it should be remembered that in those days no one did it like Max. The BBC, despite its enormous contribution to the development of ground-breaking comedy (Hancock, Spike Milligan, *Monty Python*, the list goes on), had strict, documented rules on subject matter. Many subjects were deemed taboo, the main one being sex, and Max's material dealt almost exclusively with sex. However, by using *double entendre* and innuendo, as well as sometimes leaving the audience to finish the joke, he could get away with material that less artful comedians could not. With his 'cheeky chappy' spiv persona, incredible charm and audacity, he constantly flouted conservative notions of 'good taste'. And for this he should be honoured.

Richard Pryor No one has sworn as beautifully, as rhythmically and as amusingly as Richard Pryor. After starting out as a Bill Cosby-lite comedian, Pryor evolved into an incisive social satirist, a political commentator and an amazingly versatile performer. His routines on racism and the lives of black people in the 1960s and 1970s and the words in which he described these issues were unique. In his 1979 show 'Live In Concert' (available on DVD) he discusses his problems with the law, racism and relationships and is as close to perfection as a comedy show has ever got. The outrage generated by some of his material and by his offstage personal troubles is far outweighed by the influence he has had over the last three decades since his peak.

Joan Rivers One of very few women comedians when she started out in America in the 1960s, Joan Rivers was also one of the few to be so direct, so rude and so outrageous. Her brash and outspoken stage persona, self-deprecation and caustic depiction of others' shortcomings, presented in a series of outstanding live performances, saw her mark out her own territory. Her later public image, a walking warning against cosmetic surgery, has often overshadowed her earlier achievements on the comedy stage, but it should be remembered that Joan set a standard for sheer comic bravura that few could match. She is still going strong.

Mort Sahl Although he remains little known in the UK, Sahl can be credited with starting off the whole concept of an alternative to mainstream comedy that was clever, witty, topical and delivered in an offhand manner. Mort rejected the bow-tie look of a lot of comedians in the 1950s and appeared on stage in casual clothes, often with a newspaper in his hand. He would perform as if creating the gags from the paper as he read it. He also wrote his own material with his own viewpoint, rather than relying on an anonymous gag writer, and he established the 'autobiographical' approach adopted by comedians ever since.

Victoria Wood Like Connolly before her, Britain's Victoria Wood was often, in her early career, a performer without a venue. She started off in theatres and the occasional TV slot in the 1970s with her witty songs and parochial material, which found a universal appeal – much like Peter Kay after her. As alternative comedy became more widespread and theatres and clubs began to cater for younger comedy audiences, Wood became a star, helped along by several successful TV series and sell-out tours. Her easy-going manner and feminist-influenced material were a hit, and she went on to prove herself as an astonishingly driven writer, able to work in a number of genres – songs, stand-up, plays, sketches and sitcoms. Few have matched her output and she has now earned herself a place in the pantheon of British comedy.

The following comedians and writers are mentioned more than once in this book or were interviewed specially for it.

Ed Aczel is a British 'anti-comedian' whose shambolic performance exposes the workings of stand-up comedy. He is the antithesis of 'showbiz' comedians and is more akin to Tommy Cooper.

Tony Allen was one of the first comedians to perform at London's Comedy Store in 1979. He has written, performed and taught stand-up comedy ever since and is often referred to as the 'godfather of alternative comedy'. He has also written *Attitude: the Secret of Stand-Up Comedy.*

Marcus Brigstocke is a British comedian and writer who has appeared many times on TV and radio as well as touring his own solo shows.

Arnold Brown is another veteran Scottish alternative comedian. He was one of the first at The Comedy Store in London in 1979. Unlike many other comedians, he started doing comedy when he was middle-aged.

Jimmy Carr is a writer, TV presenter and comedian whose jokes veer over the line of good taste while remaining witty, acute and very clever.

Louis CK is an American stand-up who also writes, acts and directs his own sitcom, *Louis.*

Lawrence Clark is a disabled British writer and comedian who has appeared on TV and radio as well as in many festivals and shows.

Larry David wrote *Seinfeld*, with Jerry Seinfeld, and also the improv-sitcom *Curb Your Enthusiasm*. He is a master of awkward comedy and an inspiration for a great many comedy writers.

Jill Edwards is a Brighton-based comedy teacher who has taught many comedians and been acclaimed by former students Jimmy Carr and Shazia Mirza.

George Egg, also Brighton based, is a prop comic who has been on the UK circuit for the last decade.

Dame Edna Everage (See Barry Humphries.)

Mat Fraser is a writer and comedian who has appeared on stage around the world as well as on British TV and radio. A lot of his comedy is based on his life as a disabled person.

Hannah George was the first woman to receive, in 2009, the Comedy: Writing & Performance degree at Southampton Solent University. She has since worked as a writer and as a comedian.

Lucy Greeves is a writer and the co-author, with Jimmy Carr, of *The Naked Jape: Uncovering the Hidden World of Jokes.*

Rich Hall is an American stand-up comedian and writer who has also often appeared on TV. He is the man behind the character Otis Lee Crenshaw, a parody of a country and western singer.

Neil Hamburger (See Gregg Turkington.)

Harry Hill is an instantly recognisable figure on the British circuit, with his large collar, big glasses and bald head. His routines are brilliantly structured, with a lot of reincorporation of themes, and he delights in the absurd. He is also a highly successful TV presenter.

Barry Humphries is an Australian, best known for his character Dame Edna Everage, who styles herself 'housewife superstar' and is very good at being unhelpfully rude.

Eddie Izzard is a British-born comedian who, unlike many of his countrymen, has met with some success in America. He has also performed in non-English-speaking countries and is a gifted, surreal improviser whose transvestism is often part of his act.

Zoe Lyons is a London-based comedian who has been performing for many years on stage, TV and radio.

Steve Martin is best known as an actor but was first a wildly original stand-up comedian, using music, props and magic as part of his act. His performance 'Live at the Hollywood Bowl' (1978) is one of the best and earliest stand-up shows committed to film.

The Marx Brothers started out in American vaudeville in the 1920s and went on to make a succession of superb film comedies using slapstick, banter, music, and out and out absurdity. They were masters of chaos.

Shazia Mirza is a British-born writer and comedian of Pakistani parentage who performs onstage in traditional Muslim dress and discusses social and religious taboos. She has appeared many times on radio and TV.

The Mighty Boosh is a surreal British duo whose act uses music, dance and art as well as physical and verbal comedy. They are the definitive 'cult' comedians.

Spike Milligan was another surrealist comedian. A writer, as well as a performer, he reinvented British comedy as we know it, first in *The Goon Show* on radio and then in his numerous books, films and TV programmes.

Ross Noble has been performing stand-up since his teenage years and is best known for his wildly improvised routines, which rapidly spiral into absurdity. He has a very appealing stage persona.

Emo Philips is a bizarre, awkward and slightly twisted comedian who specialises in perfect one-liners.

David Pollikett has been performing for many years as the drag queen Davina Sparkle. He is based in Brighton.

Raymond and Mr Timpkins are a British musical-comedy double act.

Chris Rock's high-energy performances, dealing with sex, drugs, politics, relationships and the African-American experience, have made him one of the most successful stand-up comedians in the world. He is also very, very funny.

Ian Saville is a socialist magician and comedian who mixes a bit of ventriloquism into his act.

Alexei Sayle was the first MC at London's Comedy Store (1979). Dressed in a tight suit and Dr Martens boots and with a skinhead haircut, he developed an aggressive, highly original stand-up style, centred on politics and philosophy.

Sarah Silverman is an American comedian renowned for her edgy comedy which plays with taboos and 'political correctness'.

Davina Sparkle (See David Pollikett.)

Gregg Turkington is the creator of Neil Hamburger, a decrepit American showbiz character who relays gross-out jokes in a deliberately shambolic manner.

Henning Wehn is a German comedian, based in London, whose comedy deals with debunking such things as football commentaries and stereotypes of German culture.

Stephen Wright is a laconic American stand-up who specialises in surreal one-liners delivered in a very monotonous voice.

Paul Zerdin is a British ventriloquist and comedian who has performed all over the world and on TV. He invented the 'human ventriloquist's dummy', which has to be seen to be believed.

2. The Language

Like any other profession, live comedy has its own language. So before we go any further, here are some terms that are regularly used in the world of live comedy and throughout this book.

Agent Someone who is best avoided and whom we can do without, who demands 15 per cent of the very little we actually earn.

Character An invention that the comedian inhabits to perform in. It offers the comedian the chance to explore other ideas, personalities and material that they may not be able to present in their own persona.

Cheque An imaginary source of revenue that is always in the post and never actually arrives at its intended destination.

Comedian A strange creature whom we encounter at gigs and towards whom we feel innate hostility because they are infinitely better at the job than we are.

Comic economics Some essential rules for performing comedy:

• Get to the punchline as soon as possible.

• If it is not essential information or the punchline, get rid of it.

• The length of the joke has to be justified by the strength of the punchline; that is, if it takes fifteen minutes to get to a feeble pun, then consider a career as perhaps a chartered accountant.

• Audiences expect a laugh every thirty to sixty seconds. If they need to hang on for a bit longer, make sure you've given them a few good short jokes previously; otherwise they lose faith.

Dying The comedian's worst nightmare, when we cannot get a laugh out of the audience – they cannot or will not relate to us and would obviously rather be elsewhere.

Encore What the audience are shouting for when you have thoroughly exhausted every last bit of material you have ever written and which you cannot possibly hope to gratify. It is also the bit on comedy DVDs when the comedian goes off the stage, pretending it's all over, then comes back a moment later.

Ethics A moral stance that indicates what a comedian will or will not say.

Euphemism Generally a mild word used to stand in for one considered too strong or offensive. In comedy also a word that has two meanings: an innocuous one and a risqué one, which the audience is clearly intended to understand, e.g. 'my girlfriend's pussy'.

Gag A joke. It can take many forms: a one-liner, a call and response or a self-contained observation, involving a set-up, a confirmation and a punchline, which is usually unexpected, thus surprising the audience into laughter.

Groupies A sexually voracious bunch of ladies apparently at liberty on the comedy circuit whom the more sadistic and experienced comedians pretend exist and whom you will never meet. So thank your lucky stars!

Heckler A member of the audience who attempts to get into the act. There are several types of heckler: the helpful heckler who joins in and enhances the evening with an amusing comment which the comedian can build on; the idiot who has a day pass from the happy house; and the drunk who has no idea who anybody is, what he (it is usually a he) is saying or even where he is. Also known as 'the asshole'.

Innuendo Language that appears relatively innocuous but implies a much ruder meaning which can be played on by the comedian.

MC The Master (or Mistress) of Ceremonies: the person who introduces the evening and brings the comedians onto the stage. They are to be treated nicely, so that (you hope) they will be nice to you. The MC is a mixture of act and intermediary.

The best MCs are the ones who just seem to chat in a funny, accessible way and whom you wouldn't mind going for a drink with.

Microphone A temperamental electrical necessity, aka a mic, with which we have to engage in order to appeal to the idiots at the back of the room.

Mic stand An impossibly complex structure in which the above sits. When we need to get the microphone out, it is as secure as a police dog's teeth on a criminal's testes. When we need to put the mic back, the stand tends to shrink down to the size of a pocket umbrella.

Microworld For a comedian, 'the way in which I see things'. Each comedian's microworld is different because it is based on their own experiences and opinions of the shared world.

Open-mic spot A five- or ten-minute space at a comedy night when new comedians can give it a go or more established comedians can try out new material. It is the place where we all start, and when we are in the audience we should remember how hard it can be.

Payment A ridiculously small amount of cash that we are expected to be grateful for – if we ever actually receive it – given after a performance, which in no way covers the expense of getting to and from the gig or even of a decent takeaway while waiting for the bus.

Persona The identity that many live performers put forward onstage. It is not a character but the performer's 'real self' heightened or exaggerated.

Pun A play on words that relies on one word's sounding like another.

Punter A member of the paying audience to whom the comedian hopes to appeal. A fickle swine at the best of times but one who attends our gigs and whose presence, multiplied, determines the difference between our getting home in a taxi or weeping in the bus shelter alone.

Reincorporation A routine – also known in the US as callbacks – in which a comedian does a couple of gags about a certain subject, then moves on to another subject, and then goes back to the initial subject intermittently. This gives the routine cohesion and involves the audience, who have to work out what the comedian is on about.

Satire A form of comedy that uses contemporary themes such as politics or celebrities in order to point out their shortcomings. Satire can be funny or not, but the main point is a moral rather than a comic one.

Set A series of gags that constitutes a performance. It can last anything from a couple of minutes to an hour. Sets can move from one observation to another quite seamlessly or consist of a series of unconnected jokes. The set is usually structured to give an impetus and drive to what the comedian is talking about.

Stand-up A solo performance usually involving a performer with a microphone, aiming to make the audience laugh every thirty seconds or so; but it has many variations. Stand-up can be performed to one person or many – however, its success is not dependent on the number of people but on the relationship between performer and audience.

Stereotype A depiction of a person or a group of people that reduces them to a single or a few characteristics, generally negative, to make fun of them.

Storming Giving a virtuoso performance that has the audience laughing with you all the way. We can never predict when it is going to happen but know when it has. The same material can storm one night and die the next. It is dependent on more than gags – it depends on time, place, atmosphere, beer and much, much more.

Timing The rhythm of a joke; the speed at which a joke is delivered; the correct number of syllables it takes to make your point and get the laugh. Also, the awareness of a comedian, when delivering a joke, that he or she should pause while the audience is still laughing before giving them more crucial information in the build-up to the next laugh. Timing is also involved in the structure of a set. The material needs to be well timed in order to give the audience opportunities to laugh at regular intervals.

Venue Often mistaken for an underground toilet but in fact much, much worse. The venue is where we are supposed to perform and will include no changing rooms, a crap PA system and a dodgy mic; inhabited by a bunch of other hopeless hopefuls that we consider our natural inferiors. And we love it!

3. Comedy

In his book *Stand-Up! On Being a Comedian*, Oliver Double writes: 'What's the secret of great comedy? Jokes.'[1] However, Tony Allen, in *Attitude: The Secret of Stand-Up Comedy*, writes: 'Jokes are merely the vehicle of stand-up comedy. The actual fuel is . . . Attitude.'[2] Perhaps there is no definitive answer. Perhaps comedy is both jokes and attitude. And more.

Both Double and Allen are widely experienced performers, writers and teachers of comedy, whose words deserve serious consideration. Arguments over comedy – how it is written, presented, understood, reviled or documented – are nothing new: they have been going on for more than 2,500 years, since the time of the ancient Greeks. Perhaps the 'secret' is like magic: it is just something being done in a way that you don't yet understand. But comedy is not magic – it is about making people laugh, not mystifying them, and if we know we can do it, we can explain how it is done in order to help others do it also.

However, there is no formula, no fail-safe recipe, for making successful live comedy; it is subject to a great many variables. Material that gets a laugh one night may not do so the next, and this is determined to a great extent by the audience and by their relationship with the comedian. If the performance is not successful, the reason could be something as trivial as the weather or the time of the week: on a rainy Wednesday night the audience may be tired and disgruntled. Or the audience may be dominated by a noisy stag party. Or the comedian may be performing badly, or may come onstage last, when the audience are laughed out. A comedian needs to develop endurance and the ability to understand why a particular performance has succeeded or failed. Performing live comedy is always a challenge and will appeal to those who like a challenge.

The greatest thing about comedy is that it is such a live thing: it is ephemeral. A joke is never the same joke twice, and we can never guarantee that the gig is going to succeed. Success is important as it gives us the reason to go on, but failure is also important: it reveals our weaknesses and, however unpalatable, it shows us what we need to improve and be aware of. We must reserve the right to fail.

This book shows you that if you want to do live comedy, and have the aptitude for it, then the best thing to do is to work hard at it. If we have the ability to make people laugh, we can look at how that can be developed into a performance. You cannot teach people to be funny, only how to make their comic performances better.

Why do we do it?

Standing on stage (or wherever) watching people enjoying the way you see the world is a powerful experience. Laughter is vital to humans because it assures us that we are alive in the world and are not taking it too seriously. Being able to elicit laughter and control it is a wonderful thing. But is there more to it than that? There are many reasons why we want to perform live comedy: it can connect with an audience in an exciting way; it is an unrepeatable experience with others whom we may never see again; and there is the sharing of a moment that we do not get in everyday life. There is a lot of truth in comedy and it can tell us something about our lives that we recognise. The art of comedy, if there is such a thing, is the ability to point out old truths in a new way or help us to recognise things that we already knew but did not realise we knew. It can change the way we think about all sorts of things, from relationships to politics.

Live comedy is the only performance mode in which the audience can reach in and directly affect the show. In the cinema, if people don't like what they hear or see, they can walk out, but their dissatisfaction does not alter the performance. Even in the theatre, the show will normally go on unchanged, irrespective of audience response. In live comedy, however, if the audience want to register their dissent, they can. And do. Live comedy entails a relationship between performer and audience, and if the audience do not like you they will let you know. It is truly a democratic process; there is no 'fourth wall', as there is in the theatre, symbolically shielding you from the audience; no cry of 'Cut!' from a director if you fluff your lines. And if you fail to get any laughs on stage, it is highly unlikely that your mum is going to meet you at the stage door and take you home for cocoa and consolation. It is a cold walk home after that.

Many people think that comedians are motivated mainly by an egotistical desire to be admired. However, that is not the case for everyone. British comedian Alexei Sayle started doing stand-up for a quite different reason: 'Every comic there's ever been wants to be liked by the audience – except me . . . I used to do comedy to be irritating.'[3] The young Eddie Izzard was more typical: after his mother died, 'a lot of affection disappeared [from his life]. If I work hard enough with the audience they give rewards.'[4] British stand-up Marcus Brigstocke performs comedy because 'stand-up is a conversation between you and the audience . . . comedy can in essence change things, it can continue an idea.'[5] The British writer and comedian Robin Ince started because he loved comedy on television: 'I did my first gig when I was 18 years old . . . and then I thought I must never do that again and then four years later started doing it again.'[6] London-based comedian David Baddiel says, 'The reason I do this job is because I've got a deep confessional drive – my comedy seems to be all about confession.'[7] So perhaps some of us are seeking absolution for our sins via the comedy stage because church is too draughty and has no bar.

Many other comedians start performing simply because they realise they can do it and that they are the funniest person in their social circle. In the course of interviewing a dozen British comedians and other industry professionals for this book, I asked them why they started doing comedy. Many said it was because they felt they had something to say. Ed Aczel started off doing stand-up because he was bored. London comedian Zoe Lyons says that she is 'a born show-off and I love making people laugh so I had to try stand-up'. Brighton-based comedy teacher Jill Edwards confirmed Zoe's point: 'It is essentially a tremendous need to show off that can be born out of many things. Many have something in their background that has led them to want to stand on stage and receive lots of love. Which is why when they die on stage it can be more crippling than it should be.'

The musical double act Raymond and Mr Timpkins had been compèring their local comedy club for a while and then 'we quickly became bored with watching white male stand-up after white male stand-up, week after week, and decided to perform something different to break up the monotony. We're a bit of a car-crash of genres but music is where we came from.' Mat Fraser's comedy career evolved almost accidentally: 'I was doing a lot of cabaret hosting and it just evolved from there . . . an act was late and I suddenly had to cover for five minutes, and it all began like that.' Hannah George enrolled on the Comedy: Writing and Performance degree at Southampton Solent University: 'I started performing comedy in the stand-up sense when I was at uni. Mostly this was due to the nature of my course and peer pressure! I'd always been a massive fan of stand-up, and having a go myself was too tempting an opportunity to miss.'

So before you go much further, you need to ask yourself the same question: why do *you* want to do it?

The comedy of the Ancients

As we've noted, the instinct to make people laugh – or just to find things funny – is part of being human, so the earliest comedy probably pre-dates civilization and it was probably fairly basic. By the fifth century BC in ancient Greece, it had become a lot more sophisticated. In particular, playwrights had launched the comic tradition of pointing out the moral or social shortcomings of others. In the comedies performed in the Greek drama festivals, the action was split in two by a *parabasis*, literally a 'stepping forward', in which the chorus directly addressed the audience. These ancient texts read like stand-up comedy. The playwrights would criticise the powerful people in the audience. For example, Aristophanes targeted the statesman Pericles and a warmongering politician called Cleon, who was the butt of many jokes. These festivals were extremely popular and aired widely held grievances. They also demonstrate how writers, although lacking political power, fought against perceived injustice. This remains part of the attraction of performing live comedy: we can have our say. As Jill Edwards says: 'There are some people who are comics because they wanted a voice. How often are we encouraged to stand up and speak?'

Greece's conquerors, the Romans, were not averse to borrowing Greek innovations. Having seen how popular comedy was, they developed their own version to keep the populace onside. But they took care to censor it: they banned the naming of names and political satire because they realised that mockery undermines the powerful (politics, then as now, was all about PR). As Roman comedy developed, it focused on more domestic issues, such as relationships. These plays were much like contemporary sitcoms: a recognisable setting and a small ensemble, with the comedy arising from social conflicts. The first-person address gradually faded away and did not come back into European comedy until the Middle Ages.

The fool and the clown

The reappearance of the individual comic spirit came in the person of the 'fool' – a character who enlivened all sorts of entertainments: morris and sword-dancing groups, plays, and festivals. He represented an anarchic – but not evil – spirit, who broke the rules and laughed at the rich and powerful. In fact a fool, or jester, might even be employed by a powerful noble or king, to entertain him, and was allowed a freedom of speech unthinkable for a courtier. Fools appear in many of Shakespeare's plays, where, despite their lowly status, they typically are more clued-up than their so-called 'superiors'. We have only to look at *King Lear* or *Twelfth Night*, for example, to find the 'wise fool', the comedian who has the gift of insight into the ways of the world and the means to express them – though not to change them. The fool gradually disappeared from both court and stage, to be replaced as a source of laughter by the visual comedy of the clown, along with the continuing development of theatrical comedy.

Music hall, variety and vaudeville

It was not until the nineteenth century, with the advent of music hall, that the solo comedian finally found an independent space to perform in. The comedians' routines alternated with songs and dance numbers. Music halls were of varying quality depending on where they were; in the centre of London, they could be quite opulent, with good-quality acts. In other parts of London, such as the East End, and in some other cities, they could be grotty dives with substandard performers playing to a generally unappreciative crowd.

As music halls declined in the twentieth century with the rise of radio and TV, variety took over. This was much more family oriented, without the bawdy songs and jokes typical of music hall. Many successful radio and TV comedians first performed in variety before progressing to more lucrative, less arduous careers.

The American counterpart of music hall was vaudeville. It too offered a varied bill, including musical numbers and comedy routines and all sorts of other entertainments, such as animal acts. With the advent of radio and the growing popularity of cinema in the 1920s, vaudeville began to decline. However, some successful screen comedians, notably Laurel and Hardy, Charlie Chaplin and the Marx Brothers, had started their careers slogging round the endless vaudeville circuit before getting their break in the cinema. Others were less lucky and continued on the vaudeville circuit doing the same act for years.

The radio and, later, TV offered the solo comedian a chance to communicate directly with the audience. Films, requiring plots, were less suited to stand-up, although some did have short comic intervals during the film for the comedians to do their thing.

The club circuits

Vaudeville and music hall were replaced by the club circuits – some in cities, others at holiday resorts, such as Blackpool in England or the Catskills in the States. The comedians who played these places would do many shows a week. Being intended for the entertainment of people enjoying their short vacations from work, these acts were a wee bit more upmarket than those on the vaudeville or music hall circuits. The comedians on the club circuits wore suits, avoided smut and dealt with standard domestic subjects that anyone could understand.

The emergence of alternative comedy

In the 1950s and 1960s, many comedians on the live circuit in the States and in Britain began to make the more profitable move into other media such as radio, TV and film. As TV became more and more central to people's lives, audiences for live comedy in theatre and clubs dwindled. They could watch it at no cost in the comfort of their homes.

Live comedy did not get a much-needed shot of adrenalin until the mid-1970s in America, when a new kind of comedian emerged, offering more youth-oriented material. Actually, this movement had got under way slightly earlier, with the opening of the Purple Onion club in San Francisco in the 1950s and the first Improv club in New York in the 1960s. But alternative comedy really came of age with the TV show *Saturday Night Live*, launched in 1975. The programme featured many well-known comedians, including Richard Pryor, Robin Williams and Eddie Murphy, and showcased the work of John Belushi, Dan Ackroyd and Chevvy Chase, who all went on to successful careers in Hollywood. It appealed to a new, young audience, who were bored with the old-school bow-tie comedians, with their gags about their wives, women drivers, foreigners and sexual phobias. They wanted to hear comedians perform material dealing specifically with pop culture and their own experiences – with the issues that affected them in their everyday lives. The style of the comedy, as well as the content, was different: it had more energy and was more aggressive, using street language and much cussing.

In the 1980s and 1990s a yet more aggressive kind of American comedy began to appear, which some critics called 'the comedy of hate'. Bill Hicks and Sam Kinnison (both deceased) were major exponents of this volatile, controversial style, which, besides being politically provocative, advocated the use of drugs and sexual experimentation. Another development was the emergence of more African-American comedians, such as Chris Rock and Dave Chappelle, who were clearly successors to the late Richard Pryor. The American live comedy circuit now has something for every taste, with prop comedians, one-line-gag experts, and mainstream acts selling out on Broadway. American comedy is a very rich industry indeed.

The Comedy Store

Meanwhile, in 1979 in London's Soho, a new venue for live comedy had opened up. Called The Comedy Store, after the Los Angeles club of that name, and inspired by that club's ideas, it offered a space where experimental new comedy could develop. The club went on to change the face of British entertainment and comedy for ever. It welcomed comedy voices that were not always male or heterosexual and promoted the idea of autobiographical comedy. Female comedians and gay comedians, among others, saw that this new 'alternative comedy' venue was a place where their own voices could be heard and where the subject matter was far removed from the stereotypical cartoon-like world of the old school. Comedians could explore and discuss their own identities and concerns onstage to a receptive, younger audience.

Alexei Sayle and Tony Allen started performing at The Comedy Store, as did the outrageous London-based comedian Julian Clary, who recognised the value of such a platform and started his career there. Clary was followed by many others and nowadays openly gay figures are hardly unusual in live comedy. For example, the gay Irish comedian Graham Norton started off doing stand-up in London and now commands a large salary for his TV work.

Comedy today

Ever since the London Comedy Store was launched, other clubs have opened and closed on a regular basis. As the 1990s gave way to the new millennium the British comedy scene became much richer and more varied. There are now comedy nights featuring different styles of comedy in most major cities and towns, and open-mic spots are not difficult to find. Comedy festivals in Brighton and Edinburgh are great events where one can see the established, the new and the strange, often on the same night. Many large British music festivals also feature cabaret tents, where the exhausted punter can wind down and listen to comedians from all over the world. Some British comedians also maintain a wider profile – on radio and TV. The style typical of most of them, once called 'alternative', is now the mainstream. Comedy clubs are opening all across Europe, while comedy continues to be a main entertainment form in the English-speaking countries.

As we have seen, comedians do comedy for different reasons. It is a portable art, it is easy to get onto the circuit and start working, and it is one of the few opportunities we have to persuade people to sit and listen to what we have to say. Comedy is a basic human instinct, which is why it has been around for at least 2,500 years and is unlikely to disappear any time soon. It deals with matters that are familiar to us – in particular, with human folly, in its manifold forms – and communicates with us directly. At its best it is a unifying force, bringing people together in laughter. There has never been a better time to be a comedian. So have a go – it's well worth the effort.

4. The Performer

In this chapter we will look at how to construct an accessible stage persona based on who we are in everyday life. We will look at the persona itself, how to structure it, the style in which we perform and who our potential audience is. We will then look at some individual cases and different approaches to performing live comedy. Female and male comedians, gay and straight comedians, disabled and able-bodied comedians and comedians from different cultures will be examined to see how identity is presented on the live comedy stage. In the following chapter we will look at the comic character: a role created by some comedians as a vehicle for their comedy. Here we are concerned with the more straightforward expression of the comedian's own persona: how to identify who we are, what we want our persona to be, what we can talk about and how to do it convincingly.

Persona: who am I?

The American comedian Jerry Seinfeld is one of the most successful stand-ups of all time. Onstage he dresses smartly and talks about the things that his audience know about – a form of stand-up called observational comedy; he observes things from his own perspective in an easy-going if slightly neurotic manner and reports his observations to the audience. Seinfeld deals with the universal rather than the specialized. He does not talk about drugs, pop music or politics but about relationships and the frustrations of everyday life, which explains his popularity. Most people can instantly recognise him as an Everyman and can relate to him or at least understand what he's talking about.

Different comedians construct their performance identity in various ways, but the process always requires some thoughtful decisions. Most comedians base their persona on themselves and their experiences, but 'heightened' – that is, they emphasise certain aspects of their true personality and their life while playing down others. For example, Seinfeld onstage may talk about the difficulties of relationships, but he does not talk about his wife and kids.

We all have the capability of being unique performers and we need to talk about our own experiences and ideas so that the audience will 'believe' and listen to us. Most of us have similar experiences, but it is the way in which the individual comedian sees these experiences and what language they use to describe them that gives the act a unique spin. For instance, we have all been to school, but each school is different and each kid has a different experience of each individual school. The one thing that we know most about is our own life. We are experts on ourselves, so it is here we have to look to find an angle that makes us different from the previous act and the next one.

Once we have worked out who we are onstage, the next question is, will the audience believe it? That is, does the material match the persona? There has to be a realistic connection between the persona onstage and the material being used in order for the comedy to be convincing to the audience. Although what the performer says may not be factually true, it has to be true to them; it has to appear that this kind of thing could well have happened to that persona. It is unlikely that a fat, bald bloke is going to be an expert womaniser or that a geeky games freak is also a top athlete. It *is* likely that the fat bloke has a direct debit for Pizzaland and the games geek has a hefty masturbation schedule. Once we have established who this comic stage persona is, an individual style can emerge.

The comedy persona application form

Filling in this 'application form' will help you to see yourself objectively so that you can start developing your stage persona.

- Who are you? Describe yourself in four words (for example, bald, angry, Northern, smoker).
- Are you generally bolshy? Angry? Resigned? Genial? Other?
- Who or what do you look like?
- Where are you from?
- What accent do you have?
- What makes your hometown interesting or different or peculiar?
- Have you moved away now? Why or why not?
- What is the material you have already written like and what impression does it give? Is it surrealist? Satirical? Smutty? Cynical? (the four S's)
- What are the subjects that you feel strongly about? Or do you not care?
- What is your language use like? Do you swear a lot? Are you overtly descriptive? Do you use a lot of street words and slang?
- What is the impression that you would like to give to an audience?
- What can you emphasise (hopelessness, drunkenness) and what should you keep quiet about (the arrest near the toilets)?
- What is it about you that is different from the others and how can you project a more individual, convincing and rounded persona?

Comic aptitude

Of course all this presupposes that the performer has comic aptitude. Aptitude is the innate ability, however unformed, to produce comic ideas and the will, discipline and imagination to develop these ideas into comic routines. This aptitude is not learned; it is an ability and it is recognisable – even some kids have it. It is the key to being creatively funny, not just 'taking the piss' or recycling other people's lines at opportune moments. Telling jokes is like telling stories; not everyone can do it. Some people are hopeless at telling either and others are just 'naturals'.

A lot of us realise we are good at making our friends laugh in the pub or other social situations and want to take it further, but performing live comedy is not the same as being funny in the pub. Being funny in the pub is more spontaneous and less rigorous, and although it is a kind of performance, there is no prepared 'act'. The pub comedian often makes jokes at the expense of those around him, which is clearly not going to work in a comedy club, where you are expected to be con-structive and demonstrate the ability to structure ideas into jokes and those jokes into a professional routine. This is aptitude in the professional sense of the word.

When interviewing students for the comedy degree at Southampton Solent University, I try to identify comic aptitude by looking at their written material. This should indicate a sufficient degree of imagination, creativity and originality but also whether they can write a simple gag. Performing live comedy requires rigour, organisation and professionalism. There are comedy standards – sometimes called comic etiquette – and audience expectations that are long established, and we need to acknowledge these. The audience expects to laugh at regular intervals, at best every thirty seconds to a minute – two minutes is pushing it somewhat; they expect a degree of professionalism; and they do not know you (unlike your mates in the pub), so you need to understand what they will go along with and establish a relationship with them.

Recognising comic aptitude

Knowing we can make people laugh is a good start and indicative of comic aptitude but it is not the same thing as live comedy, so ask yourself:
- Am I funny in everyday life?
- Can my sense of humour translate into performance?
- How do I put myself across in a comedic manner?
- When am I funniest?
- About what?

Who should not perform live comedy?

Before we go any further, we ought to address the uncomfortable issue of people who have no business on a comedy stage. A lot of what follows is implicit in the guidelines in this chapter, but just to make things clear, here are a few types of people who should not attempt a career in comedy.

The Piss Taker 'Taking the piss', for want of a better term, is not comedy. Some people are good at this in their own social circles, but it does not translate onto the comedy stage. It is group humour and aims to get laughter from the perceived shortcomings of others, but it is not a structured performance. After all, an audience is not going to submit to being mocked by someone they do not know. Taking the piss is not constructive and needs a target who is, preferably, at a disadvantage; it's a form of bullying. It is also exclusive and not inclusive: live comedy is at its best when the comedian discusses shared experiences and includes the audience in the moment. Targeting someone excludes them from the moment, and there is a risk that the audience may start to side with the victim rather than with the person onstage, which means that the comedian will lose the gig. To perform live comedy effectively, we need to communicate with the audience, to get them onside and included in our microworld. Pick your targets carefully.

The Class Clown The Class Clown never knows when to shut up, constantly demands attention and goes for the gag at every single opportunity. They become so embroiled in their own antics that they fail to realise how annoying others find them. Comedy requires structure and discipline as well as improvisational skills. It is hard work. There is also a time and a place for it. The Class Clown fails to realise this and, more often than not, isn't that funny anyway.

The Deluded It is important to distinguish the comedy fan from the comedian. Liking comedy a lot is not enough. You need skill, confidence, aptitude and imagination. Just because someone has a stock joke for every occasion ('as the actress said to the bishop . . .') does not mean that an audience wants to hear recycled corny material from an inferior performer. People who smoke pipes or who are called Uncle Malcolm tend to fall into this category.

Knowing when to give up

In live comedy it is important to get balanced feedback from people you trust, people who you know have your own interests and enthusiasms at heart. Do not ask your mum what she thought of your gig: she will obviously love it. Do not ask your cynical mate in the pub: he will obviously hate it. Take along someone who knows enough about comedy to assess fairly how you did onstage. You will be way too nervous and preoccupied to deliver a balanced verdict on your early performances, so a clear-headed and supportive friend is useful.

Sadly, not everyone has clear-headed and supportive friends and so they do not get the advice they so desperately need, which in some cases is to be advised to give up. There is a big difference between the audience laughing with you (going along with the gags as you have directed) and laughing at you (watching you make a complete idiot of yourself onstage and enjoying your discomfort). Most audiences want you to be good, but there are some that enjoy nothing more than the spectacle of some hopeless wannabe comedian dying on his arse. (In the 1980s, the audience at Malcolm Hardee's Tunnel Club in south London became notorious for heckling off both good and bad acts.) The truly hopeless comedian struggles on without the benefit of advice and is encouraged by the sound of laughter, any laughter, failing to realise that it is based on his or her own ineptitude. The audience have to feel comfortable with a comedian and buy into the comedian's microworld. Laughter at the hopeless case betrays a failure to convince. Go back to the day job.

Style

The style of the comedian develops alongside the persona: the *style* is the way in which something is done; the *persona* is who is doing it. The two should be harmonious. The surreal American stand-up Emo Philips does not talk about being a great womanizer because we would never believe him; instead, he discusses his strange experiences, which match his weird persona in his own unique style. Chris Rock talks from the perspective of a politically angry black guy from Brooklyn about the things that black people – as well as white people – understand all too well. This is his style.

The way that we speak, what we speak about and how we feel about it all contribute to our own individual style. Some comedians have created a style way ahead of their time. Lenny Bruce, for example, was renowned for his originality, taboo busting and improvisation skills; Richard Pryor, for his unflinching honesty and clever use of language; Joan Rivers, for introducing brash female comedy at a time when women were hardly noticeable on the comedy scene; and Bill Hicks, for his anarchic comedy, which was underpinned by a strong sense of morality. What all these comedians have in common is that they speak (or spoke) in their own authentic language, with conviction and imagination, about the things that they know and understand best. Their material is imbued with passion and expressed with spontaneity and verbal brio. Pryor may not have been as urbane as Bob Hope, but no one said 'motherf****r' quite like him.

How does a comedian discover and develop an individual style? Comedy teacher Jill Edwards gets her students to look for their 'inner comic' and British comedian and writer Tony Allen calls it simply, brilliantly, 'Attitude'. The style of the comedian – name (or stage name), appearance, delivery and material – must be recognisable and distinctive, so that the audience know what to expect. The style can even be irritating to some audiences, so long as it is unique. Style is deliberately nurtured but it is not pretence. The audience may not think that Emo Philips is the epitome of cool, but he has a style all of his own (perhaps because nobody else could do it).

A good way to scrutinise your own style is to record your performances, which is easy with digital technology so widely available and cheap. This is a great help as you can analyse them at your leisure. Buy a digital voice recorder; these are inexpensive and can store hours of material. The British surrealist comedian Ross Noble, who improvises a great deal of material every night, records all of his sets, then plays them back to see what worked and what did not. Filming helps to analyse the physical aspects of the performance, although many of us do not like watching ourselves, as it can be a faintly embarrassing experience. Film is, however, invaluable for detecting nuances, body language, verbal glitches and twitches – or even accidental catchphrases that could be worth including in future sets. Looking back on this footage, like listening, should always be done either alone or with close friends, but it is here that we can begin to locate our performance style.

Watching yourself on film

When watching your own comedy act on film, ask yourself the following:

- Do I move about too much?
- Do I look static?
- What do I do with my hands?
- What am I doing well and can it be improved?
- Are these jokes 'truthful'?
- How do I come across to the audience?
- How would I describe what I do in as few words as possible?
- Am I funny?

Stage names

No matter what kind of comedy you do, no matter what style, you need the audience to remember you. Having a memorable or unusual name can help. Stage names can even influence the way an audience responds to a comedian. Some comedians are lucky and already have memorable names: Mort Sahl, Eddie Izzard and Spike Milligan are different without being hard to remember. A short name is often best: Chris Rock, Rich Hall and Ken Dodd are punchy. Less familiar names, such as Ed Aczel or Demetri Martin, are worth keeping. These may be initially tricky to recall after one performance, but they look striking when written down and are sufficiently unusual to stand out so that people will remember them. A one-syllable first name with a two-syllable surname works rhythmically: Dame Edna, Joan Rivers, Steve Martin.

If you form part of a double act or a small group, choosing a good stage name offers more opportunities. Consider the rhythmic flow of 'Morecambe and Wise' ('Morecambe' itself – after the town – being John Eric Bartholomew's own stage name). The Marx Brothers could exploit their family identity in their stage name. Such novelties as 'The League of Gentlemen' or 20th Century Coyote (Rik Mayall and Ade Edmondson's first comedy duo) are a bit more rock and roll.

It is important to pick up on anything that will distinguish you from the comedians who go onstage before and after you. Adapting your name or using a nickname (e.g. 'Spike' Milligan) is one thing, but going out under a joke name might prove wearing. 'David Suggestible-Hyphen' may have initial comic appeal, but this could wear off after a few years. Remember: if you choose a stage name you will be stuck with it, so choose it carefully.

What's in a name?

You may be able to adapt your own name for your stage name.

- Do you have a nickname like Spike?
- Is there anything about your name that makes it stand out, like Louis CK or Emo Philips?
- Can you emphasise it or twist it slightly to make it more memorable? Can you use other family surnames?

Comedy fashion

Audience members assess us first on our names, then on how we look and then on our content and delivery. Our society is a superficial one; we like to make instant value judgements based on appearances and this includes comedy acts. Traditionally comic theatre has used costume to symbolise the nature of a character – e.g. shabby clothes = low character, nice clothes = rich character – thus removing the need for complex back stories. We can draw on this principle when performing live comedy. What we wear can indicate to the audience what to expect, in some cases being so strikingly visual that it sticks in the memory. Billy Connolly is well known for his wild hair and beard; Harry Hill's massive collars, creepers and bald head make him instantly recognisable; and Sarah Silverman's black stage outfits are both striking and visually appealing.

But this was not always so. It was not until the 1950s that Mort Sahl walked onstage wearing casual clothes instead of the penguin suit much beloved of the more orthodox comedians. Since the 1960s comedians have tended to dress much as their audiences do. There are exceptions, as the costume can become a gimmick. Steve Martin used to wear a white suit (and an arrow through his head), which had a clownish appeal, and British comic magician Tommy Cooper always used to wear a fez and a shabby suit. Other comedians are noted for their sartorial elegance and are no strangers to bespoke tailors: Lenny Bruce wore classic Italian suits; British comedian Vic Reeves is never without a foppish suit; and Joan Rivers is always impeccably turned out.

It may sound ridiculous to worry about what trousers to wear for a five-minute slot in a dingy cellar, but it is part of an overall well-thought-out strategy to project a coherent onstage persona. Clothes can be deliberately chosen to influence people's perceptions so you need to see them as another part of the act that needs consideration. There is a difference between costumes and stage clothes, however: most of the outfits mentioned above (except those of Hill, Martin and Cooper) are simply stage clothes and are similar to what they would wear on a night out. Costumes are there to project the character, like the stained dinner jacket of American 'nightclub entertainer' Neil Hamburger, or Emo Philips's entire eccentric wardrobe and haircut. Whatever you choose to wear will inevitably help audience expectations. Using the same costume, as well as the same photo and type font for publicity, presents an image that shows people you are serious and professional in approach.

Outfitting yourself

When choosing your stage outfit, ask yourself the following questions:
- What do I wear normally?
- What does it indicate?
- Is it neutral or making a statement?
- What statement do I want to make?
- Will the clothes I wear communicate the persona effectively to the audience?

Who is the audience?

In order for a comedian to connect with an audience, they need to talk about the things that the audience can relate to. When developing a stage persona a comedian should always have a particular audience in mind:
- Who is likely to be listening?
- Whom would I prefer to perform to?
- Who will best relate to my material?
- How will different audiences relate to the persona I am putting forward?

Once on the stage, a comedian has to build a relationship with the audience through a shared frame of reference – that is, to talk about the things that they understand or at least recognise. There is no point in doing twenty minutes on *Buffy the Vampire Slayer* or *The X-Files* to an audience of old-age pensioners who are unlikely to have ever watched the programmes in the first place. They would swiftly become bored and confused. The key thing is to talk about things that most people in that particular audience will relate to.

In general after a few gigs we realise who 'gets' our material and who does not. So even though we do not want to turn down work, we have to be careful that the targeted audience will have some relationship to what we are doing onstage. It may not be the material; it may be the performance style or language (swearing!), so we need to be able to adjust the intensity and velocity of delivery to accord with the audience. After all, we are there to entertain them, and if we know what the regular crowd are like we can adjust our material to suit them. Attending a typical event at that venue can help in this respect.

Picking your audience

When considering your audience, remember to ask yourself these questions:

- Whom do I really want to talk to? Peers? Students? Middle-aged people?
- Who will 'get' it and who won't? Are regular audiences likely to 'get' all of the material or does some of it require specialised knowledge?
- What kind of places have acts similar to mine? Is it the right gig and audience for me?
- How am I different to them? What is it about my act that makes me different from the others on the circuit?

Microworlds

Another key factor in a comedian's persona is their 'microworld'. A microworld is the world the individual comedian lives in while onstage. For example, Chris Rock talks about his own life: about growing up black in a predominantly white neighbourhood and going to a white school; about what life is like in Afro-American communities and how black people behave within them. His descriptions of and opinions on these experiences introduce the audience to his microworld. The picture of this microworld is built up gradually as the jokes draw the audience in, and each joke reveals more information about the way in which he sees things and, more importantly, how he feels about them. When we see Rock subsequently we can locate ourselves in the familiar territory of his microworld; we know pretty much what to expect from him and we learn a bit more about life from his perspective.

Every comedian's microworld is different. They can be odd or fascinating; they can reflect our own experiences or temporarily help us forget our everyday lives. Well-established comedians build a relationship with a certain percentage of their audience who come back to see them time and again because they feel comfortable in their microworlds.

With so much comedy available – on the live circuit, DVD or the Internet – we can access many microworlds: surreal, cynical, smutty, satirical, to name just a few. Most surreal comedians live in bizarre microworlds with their own catchphrases and strange characterisations, almost a mirror image to our own real world. One example is Ross Noble, whose comedy spirals off at odd tangents yet still makes sense. At the other extreme are comedians such as Louis CK who live in the everyday world and whose reference points are in the supermarket, on the bus or at home watching daytime TV. However, all comedians have their own unique way of looking at things. It may not necessarily be like ours – which is why we like to listen to them, to see the world differently, as they do.

Where will you live?

In deciding what your own microworld is, ask yourself these questions:

- How do I see the world?
- Is it a gentle or harsh world view?
- Is it a world made up of everyday observations or something more unusual?
- How will the audience relate to it?
- Does the microworld connect to my persona effectively?

Back to square one

In most comedy – both stand-up and sitcom – a large part of the humour comes from the failure of humans to learn from their mistakes. Sitcom offers many good examples of this. Homer Simpson never learns; nor does Larry, in *Curb Your Enthusiasm*. They commit an error and experience the fallout from it. The audience are shown the consequences of Homer's or Larry's actions and see that this is not a good way to behave. Then, typically, in the following episode the character must return to square one. The repercussions of previous actions are swiftly forgotten and the character is free to blunder all over again. This gives the character comic vitality and mileage, so that they have more adventures in them. Think of Laurel and Hardy and the comic violence they endure in one scene, only to be perfectly well in the next one.

Similarly, in live comedy, despite all the comedian's stories of blundering and the implied learning from their mistakes, this never happens. The microworld must be set back to square one at the end of each anecdote or joke. The comic persona must not be overtly affected or transformed, for any extended period of time, by the experiences that they undergo. It is the repetition of the comedian's fundamental flaws, played out in front of the audience, that creates the comedy. If that flaw were somehow rectified, the comedian would no longer be as entertaining. The comic essence is the inability to learn from mistakes, because mistakes are funny. As the great Peter Cook once said, 'I have learned from my mistakes, and I am sure I can repeat them exactly.'

Being liked

Once we have established that we can make the audience laugh and that they can relate to what we are saying, we also have to present ourselves in a positive light. No matter what the comedian's style, even if it's hostile or shocking, there still needs to be something for the audience to like or enjoy – something that will generate some positive feelings. This is not the ingratiating style much abused by entertainers such as Jay Leno – the 'Hey, I'm just like you only with a Rolls-Royce' approach, which can be annoying or alienating. There has to be a genuine relationship between audience and performer, based on trust and empathy: trust in the comedian's ability to make us laugh; empathy in that we temporarily see and suffer the world as they do. Although a little self-deprecation can get the audience to empathise with the performer, he or she cannot become so pathetic as to lose the sympathy of the audience. The element of 'liking', rather than sympathy, must be retained; otherwise the persona becomes annoying.

Not all comedians, however, seek to be stroked by the audience. On the Seinfeld DVD collection, various cast members discuss the first time they saw Larry David, the show's co-creator, doing stand-up. He would come onstage, look at the audience, shake his head and walk off. Or he would verbally insult them and then walk off. Bill Hicks famously instructed his audience, 'If anyone here is in advertising or marketing – kill yourselves!' This is perhaps not the best way to ingratiate oneself with the audience, but it does make for legendary status.

Glaswegian comedian and magician Gerry Sadowitz has spent much of his career being actively hostile towards the audience and his microworld has been characterised by aggression and negativity. Sadowitz's sets of bilious, brilliantly crafted material are based on contempt and disappointment with his own life and the expectations of others. He greeted the audience at the Montreal Comedy Festival with the line 'Hello Moose F****rs!' – after which he was punched to the floor by an irate audience member. Despite the negativity, the quality of Sadowitz's material and his energetic performance style make him compulsive viewing.

Sadowitz is not the only comedian to be walking a fine line between comic relief and physical assault. British comedian and actor Keith Allen was assaulted by a soldier when on tour with the Comedy Store team in the 1980s. He had made a disparaging remark about the Falklands, and a soldier chose to register his dissent with a well-placed right hook. Allen was not one to shy away from confrontation during performances: he is reputed to have set fire extinguishers off and thrown darts at the audience. Although dangerous, such an approach can actually help a comedian's reputation. In 2007 Australian comedian Jim Jeffries was assaulted by an irate audience member in Manchester over his exceptionally foul-mouthed material – an incident that was swiftly put out on YouTube. The clip has had over 600,000 hits. Not an approach to be recommended, however.

Uncut, pure contempt for the audience does alienate people.

To have a chance of success, it must be part of the act; if we start with the understanding that this is the comedian whose act involves disliking the audience, we can cope with it. However, if the act is simply a stream of abuse directed at one individual, or a spontaneous outburst of hatred, the comedian may have trouble escaping from the venue. British comedian and presenter Mark Lamarr recalls an occasion when he died onstage at The Comedy Store in London, and retaliated with contempt. Fellow comedian Paul Merton, who had witnessed the incident, told him that 'it was stunning to see somebody die who looked at the audience with such complete contempt ... "How f*****g dare you not laugh at this? This is genius! Don't try and sit there and tell me this isn't funny. I know this is funny."' Again, perhaps not the best approach. If the audience do not go with it, get off the stage.

How far to go

You need to understand what kind of material and approach you can get away with. Ask yourself:

- Is it true to my stage persona?
- Is it too edgy for some audiences?
- Is it clear that this is just an act?
- How can I modify it if it goes wrong?
- Can anyone sneak up behind me?

Cool? Forget it!

Although live comedy has often been dubbed the 'new rock and roll' by lazy hack writers, it isn't. They don't really mean this. Rock stars are there to act out our base fantasies for us – fantasies of drugs, money, sex and more drugs. Comedians operate differently: they reveal the kind of faults and failures that the audience can relate to. Comedy is often about weakness: weakness of will, weakness in the face of power, weakness in spite of ourselves. It is about doing or saying the wrong thing, being frustrated or making a fool of ourselves. This is not cool. Although sitcoms can be aspirational (*Friends* or *Sex and the City*, for example) a lot of live comedy is about being rubbish at life (American stand-ups like Louis CK or Seinfeld) or angry about it (Richard Pryor, Bill Hicks, Chris Rock). Cool is not good for comedy.

Although there are cool, sexy or glamorous comedians – Sarah Silverman or Rob Newman, for example – they still elaborate on their faults or discuss things that affect all of us. Being a rock star is too distant from the audience's experiences and develops a different kind of audience-performer relationship which is not good for comedy. They are not like us. Whereas, with some notable exceptions, most comedians are just like us. They can, however, use cool for comic purposes; they can create a persona who has a higher opinion of themself than the audience does. We, the audience, are well aware of the persona's pretensions and we follow their progress into disaster as they make a mess of things through their lack of self-awareness. Although this is quite difficult to pull off and veers more towards character- than persona-based comedy, a stand-up can relate a story of a situation that went wrong because of trying to be cool and get a laugh. Most people have tried to impress someone with assumed cool, and it has often ended in embarrassment. This is good material for live comedy.

Who can perform live comedy?

Anyone can perform live comedy despite gender, sexuality, race or physical characteristics so long as they can structure ideas and opinions into jokes and relate them convincingly to an audience – in other words, have comic aptitude.

Does age matter?

Bill Hicks first did it at 15. So did Ross Noble. Arnold Brown was in his late 40s, and Ken Dodd is 85 and still doing it. Some people do it once and never do it again and some people can never get enough of it. So when anyone asks, 'When is a good time to start performing live comedy?' the answer is anytime. A person of any age can do it. If the desire, discipline and aptitude are there and you can make other people laugh in social situations, then it is not a massive step to trying it out at a low-key gig.

One of the things that have changed in popular culture over the last couple of decades is that the life expectancy of performers is now longer than it has ever been and many people who started off in the 1960s are still at it: in music, the Rolling Stones, The Who; in acting, Robert Redford and Dame Judi Dench; in general entertainment, Larry King and Bruce Forsyth. The same applies to comedy. Comedian George Burns was still performing after reaching 100 and Jackie Mason, one of the greatest American comedians of all time, has been a 'senior citizen' for well over a decade.

So if you want to do it, no matter how old you are, the only thing stopping you is you. And getting your Zimmer frame onto the stage.

Women and live comedy

In the world of comedy, only one out of ten performers is a woman. This may seem very few, but compared with the situation twenty years ago it's a significant improvement. This continuing gender imbalance should not inhibit women from getting up and giving live comedy a go. For Julian Hall, author of *The Rough Guide to Cult Comedy* and the comedy reviewer for the British newspaper the *Independent*, things are changing both in numbers and in style: 'There are more women performing stand-up than ever before, and people like Sarah Millican will help show that there is another generation coming through – it's not all about Jo Brand and Victoria Wood. Women are still regarded with suspicion by audiences, but I have found that it is actually other women who are often the most circumspect about the abilities of female comics.'

Women comedians do feel that there is more pressure on them than on men and that men are looking at them not only as comedians but also as women, so they feel that they have a harder job. Julian also sees some venues and audiences as difficult regarding attitudes towards women: 'There are still venues that are perceived as women-unfriendly and of course this is as much to do with the audience as the MC or the visiting acts.' For a woman, in particular, it is a smart move to visit any potential venues if possible to gauge the reaction of the audiences to female acts before deciding to perform there. Voluntarily performing at an unwelcoming venue and for people who are predisposed to dislike you is simply not worth the effort.

Some women comedians claim that the prejudice they encounter from some male audience members reflects the situation in society at large – men are encouraged to be funny and it can be a valuable social asset, therefore we are used to it. For a woman to be funny is viewed by some people as 'unladylike', so we are less used to it. Men often feel undermined by women who are funnier than they are. When asked how women are viewed in live comedy, British Asian comedian Shazia Mirza said that women were perceived 'generally as unfunny. Or not as funny as men'. Just as in everyday life. Zoe Lyons has been performing stand-up since 2003 and has done all kinds of TV, radio and comedy festivals since then. When asked what women should watch out for in stand-up she replied with the following (see overleaf):

I think many of the pitfalls are the same for anybody in stand-up, male or female. But as a female stand-up you will at some point come across some audience members who are still not altogether up to speed with the idea that women can be stand-ups. I had it just last month: I walked to the mic and a bloke shouted out, 'Oh God . . . it's a girl!' Didn't bother me, I quite like being called a girl at my age, to be honest. My theory is, it doesn't matter what job you do – you will encounter idiots. I think my material is non gender-specific. I don't really talk about being a woman per se. My advice would be to be yourself and do your thing.

Hannah George was the first female graduate from Southampton Solent University's Comedy: Writing and Performance degree course in 2009. Since graduating she has been performing stand-up on the UK comedy circuit and writing for the BBC.

Hannah thinks women are perceived unfairly in live comedy and that it remains a male-dominated environment: 'Of all the people I've risen through the ranks with in stand-up, very few of the people I know who have done really well have been women. Despite the fact of lots of them being funnier than the guys who have done really well. I think the lifestyle puts a lot of women off, so not as many actually try it. Women are still seen as speciality acts.' However, the trick is to keep performing and not to quit. Hannah says, 'I think it's very easy to say, "Well, I haven't done as well as a bloke because I'm female," but I guess you're never sure what's holding you back in stand-up and what propels you forward. I think audiences are slightly more difficult to win over as a female comedian.'

So it is important for women not to use this as a convenient excuse for not going over well. Any comedian, male or female, always has to be honest about why the act did well or why it did not and stick to what we believe is right for us.

Jill Edwards has been running comedy workshops in London and Brighton for several years and counts Jimmy Carr and Shazia Mirza as two of her former students. She has this to say about the gender balance in her classes: 'I get a good deal of women on the course, never more than half, usually a third. Women are equally funny but they don't usually have the innate confidence that men have. It takes women longer to get comfortable onstage . . . Women don't seem to feel they have a right to speak in the way that a man does.' So it is important for a woman to feel and sound confident on the stage. To help with this, get as much information about the venue and audience as possible and make sure it is suitable for you and for your material. Be confident: you are funny! In Zoe's words: 'Be yourself and do your thing.' If you follow these guidelines, you should not find gender an issue.

Sexuality

The representation of homosexual figures in live comedy has altered radically over the last thirty years. Previously in both sitcom and stand-up, any gay sexuality was implied rather than made explicit. 'Gay' characters tended to be ineffectual or were effeminate or were viewed either as suspicious or as deviant.

This has changed significantly. Gay characters have often been camp, but campness does not necessarily imply gay sexuality. Camp has always been used as a comic tool: if we look at the successful sitcom *Frasier*, both Frasier and Niles are what we can call 'hetero-camp' figures. The films of the American director John Waters, such as *Cry Baby* and *Hairspray,* are outrageously camp but they have no overtly homosexual content. Camp can also be used by heterosexual stand-up comedians: if we look at the success of Michael

Macintyre, we can see that camp can go a long way even within the confines of a comedian's persona. When it comes to comic characters, anything is possible, as we can see in Dame Edna Everage, the Australian 'housewife superstar'. Camp is simply an exaggerated performance, as are pantomime and certain drag acts. In some cases, of course, the camp element is linked to homosexual identity. The gay San Franciscan comedian Scott Capuro is camp but also very open about his sexuality.

British comedian Zoe Lyons's performances are characterised by high-energy riffs on the absurdities of everyday life, although she also discusses her lesbian sexuality at some gigs, depending on whether or not it is appropriate to what she is talking about at the time: 'I don't feel I have to. I think most of the audience can probably guess I am gay anyway by looking at me. I have a collection of trainers that would be the envy of any teenage boy.' This is testament to comedy audiences' general acceptance of different voices. But such a relaxed approach to dealing with her sexuality does not always go to plan, as Zoe explains: 'I have had the experience where I have mentioned it halfway through a gig and there has been a noticeable change in the audience's reaction to me.' This is unusual, however. As far as hecklers are concerned, 'I do get them but they are pretty rare, to be honest, and I have learnt to deal with them.'

So we can choose to represent our sexuality in different ways. Sexuality is a very significant part of our identity, and if we are presenting ourselves in a 'heightened' manner, as a persona, it is difficult to ignore the fleshly side of our lives. Some comedians, like Scott Capuro, are out and out gay, flamboyant and outrageous; others, such as Zoe, are more subtle or circumspect.

Disability

On most live comedy circuits now there are disabled comedians who show that if a disabled person has the desire and aptitude to be funny onstage, any barrier to achieving this is imaginary. This is demonstrated by the careers of disabled British comedians Mat Fraser and Laurence Clark. Mat has been performing cabaret and burlesque (as well as being an actor and musician) around the world for fifteen years – in the States, Europe and Australia. He says it took ten of those years before he felt he had got a solid act together. A regular on the BBC *Ouch!* podcast, which deals with the lives and experience of disabled people, Mat was born with phocomelia (a kind of deformity) in both arms, and he performs both with and without prosthetics. He started performing live comedy quite by accident; he had been hosting at cabarets for a while when one night 'an act was late and I suddenly had to cover for five minutes . . . and it all began like that.' Like many other comedians Mat realised he could be funny while he was in school, using comedy partly as a defence mechanism. 'I've always enjoyed making people laugh and telling stories that hold their attention, because sometimes if they got bored they would go back to bullying me.' He notes that it is better to make people laugh 'at what you say, rather than because you look funny and weird to them – even though a lot of my comedy is about that difference.'

Mat incorporates his experiences into his act and also addresses the audience's attitudes towards disability. He says that the initial reactions to his disability were varied and that disabled comedians have to address an audience's worries and concerns so that people can relax. He notes that although there is tension in some audiences when he first appears onstage, they will quickly get onside when 'you hit it right, you get a big opening laugh and they decide to like you.' There is nothing Mat would not joke about: 'Every single subject is open to comedy, it's all about how you tell it, where you're coming from, and the context in which you do it.' As for advice for any disabled person doing live comedy, he says, 'I think the time is ripe for good disabled comedians' and that there are some 'current gaps in a potentially lucrative market [including] really good short people'. There's room, he says, for 'all of us, really, as long as, like any other comedians, you have something that is individually yours'.

Laurence Clark started off wanting to be a comedy writer but soon realised that the best way to get his material noticed was by getting out and performing it himself. Laurence has cerebral palsy, and this influences much of his comedy. It took him about a year before he felt he had a professional act, and he performed his 'All-Star Charity Show' at the Edinburgh Fringe in 2003. Since then he has been performing his one-man shows at Edinburgh as well as featuring on TV and radio and he appears on the BBC *Ouch!* blog.

Laurence revealed that he was originally inspired by Mat Fraser, who showed him that it was possible for disabled people to make a career out of comedy. He was also inspired by Dave Gorman, a British comedian who uses slides and video in his stand-up, demonstrating, Lawrence says, that 'it doesn't just have to be one person standing on a stage. This inspired me to develop a way that I could perform stand-up.' Laurence found a way of both overcoming and utilising his disability, and he says that people have very different expectations about his act. 'Some people think that my act is going to be worthy in some way and not particularly funny. Sometimes people say to me, "You don't do comedy about disability, do you?", as if it's going to be really depressing.' For the live comedians, it is all a matter of talking from your own point of view and about your own experiences: 'All stand-up comics use aspects of themselves and their experiences to create material, and I don't see why disabled comics should be any different.'

Although comedy has changed over the last thirty years as to what is and is not acceptable, Laurence says there are few taboos. However, this depends on context: 'There is a big difference in what is acceptable on stage and on TV.' For Laurence, like Mat and many other comedians, there are no subjects that are off-limits; it is the intention behind the joke that is important, rather than the subject matter. 'I don't think there's any particular subject I wouldn't make a joke about, but it depends on what you are trying to say through that joke.'

Neither Mat Fraser nor Laurence Clark sees his disability as preventing him from performing live comedy; if anything, their condition has given them experiences and angles that few other comedians could replicate. For Laurence, the main thing for any disabled person who wants to try live comedy is to 'get as much practice as you can. I started doing small disability arts cabarets like DaDaFest before moving on to comedy venues and this gave me a safe environment to try out material.'

Multicultural comedy

Today's increasingly multicultural societies are reflected, as in other areas of life, on the live comedy stage. More and more comedy bills feature folks from different regions, religions and ethnicities, and the way these identities are presented can vary enormously. In the States some of the most influential comedians of the last few decades have come from the African-American community and have used the comedy stage to convey their different experiences. We have only to think of the comedian-political activist Dick Gregory, the incredibly popular Bill Cosby, the radical genius Richard Pryor, the versatile film star Whoopee Goldberg (very underrated as a stand-up comedian) and the world-famous Chris Rock to see the range and magnitude of this trend. Many black comedians move easily between stage, TV and films: Eddie Murphy started his career doing stand-up on *Saturday Night Live* aged nineteen and went on to make a series of hugely successful movies. Things have certainly changed since the early years of the twentieth century, when white comedians 'blacked up' to get cheap laughs.

British-Asian comedians have become much more noticeable in the last twenty years, particularly after the success of the BBC's crossover sketch programme *Goodness Gracious Me*, which gave an original and fresh take on British-Asian culture – something that many white viewers recognised but were not very conversant with. Since then, the various protagonists in the show have diversified in many ways, but the show itself has had the lasting effect of demonstrating that British-Asian performers could be as funny, self-deprecatory and acerbic as anyone else. And other British-Asian comedians have emerged in their wake. Although their presence is still fairly small on the live comedy scene, they provide their own insights into aspects of shared British culture. The 'otherness' of a performer can actually work to their advantage in creating a memorable persona – one that potentially will contrast with other comedians appearing in the same gig and that will offer an individual angle, making the act interesting.

British-Asian comedian Shazia Mirza is one of the most distinctive stand-ups, having an entirely original take on everyday life in the UK. When she started performing live comedy in September 2000, there were few comedians from whom she could take a cue. 'All I knew was what I had seen on TV growing up, like *The Two Ronnies*, Dick Emery, Kenny Everett, Frankie Howerd. I liked all the gay men, even though I didn't know they were gay.' When she started doing stand-up she didn't know that much about it: 'I had never watched live stand-up comedy before I started performing it. Then when I

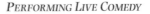

started doing it I became inspired by the comedy of Richard Pryor.' When asked if she had ever come across particular difficulties with her ethnicity on stage she says, 'There have been many difficulties for me. Saying things on stage and then wondering afterwards if I really do think, or honestly feel, what I have just said? Being myself. Telling jokes for the sake of getting a laugh, no matter how bad the joke.' Shazia's success is due not only to the way she represents her cultural identity on stage but also to hard work and some inspiring and insightful comedy, and her identity is no longer such a dominant feature now that more British-Asian comedians are arriving on the comedy circuit.

'Anti-German stereotypes are a socially acceptable form of racism,' says Henning Wehn, the self-styled 'German Comedy Ambassador to Britain'. Wehn has been performing stand-up since 2003, when he appeared at a Laughing Horse night in London. Before becoming a comedian, Henning worked in marketing – experience that helped him to realise that as a comedian he had a unique selling point. He recognised that all comedians need an angle and that 'there must be something there first that you can sell'.

The initial reaction to Henning's performances was 'a certain degree of puzzlement' at a German doing stand-up comedy. At the outset audience expectations 'were quite low'. He has always been aware that certain members of the audience will view him in a stereotypical way and that 'you have to win them round quickly'. When he started, this was a problem. One theoretical option was to go onstage and say, 'I am from Sweden.' But he realised that this would be dishonest; and anyway being German was what the act was about. His material is social commentary, playing with the stereotype people have of humourless Germans: 'Stereotypes make life easy and therefore make comedy easier to write. To have a unique viewpoint that has nothing to do with stereotypes is harder to write but it is doable.' Henning later got a break as a TV pundit during the 2006 soccer World Cup: 'Deciding to do this was the best decision of my life.'

Stand-up in Germany has not had such a rich history as in English-speaking countries, and he was originally inspired by seeing British comedians on TV. This has been an advantage: 'I am very much a British comic . . . the only comics I'd ever seen were British, therefore I'm familiar with the way the British comedy mind works.' Henning did not start doing stand-up until he had moved to Britain, so he learned the British idiom. His nationality is his angle, but ultimately he would prefer to be known not as a German comedian but 'as a very good comic who just happens to come from Germany'.

Anti-comedy

The Dutch comedian Hans Teeuwen has established himself as a remarkable performer around Europe. He specialises in setting up a comic situation then taking it to logical extremes, going 'beyond comedy'. If the audience is onside, they will go along with it to see what happens (which they do now that he has established himself). It can take a while to get adjusted to his unconventional style when seeing him for the first time, as it is odd – not quite stand-up comedy, but still funny. He speaks with a strong Dutch accent and comes across as nervous and uncertain. Teeuwen is good at being bad, rather than simply being bad; he is an experienced performer who knows exactly what he is doing. He performs bizarre musical diversions on the piano and extended monologues which stretch the audience's credulity. It is this that sets him apart and has earned him a reputation for being an 'anti-comedian'. It has to be seen to be believed. Anti-comedy, such as Teeuwen's, is becoming more prevalent at comedy festivals now.

Although it breaks the rules and conventions given in this book, anti-comedy should not be confused with carelessness or inexperience. Unlike the novice comedian, the anti-comedian knows the rules and deliberately plays with them. One notable British anti-comedian is Ed Aczel. In one of his appearances at the Edinburgh Festival Fringe, Aczel recited a list of 'what a stand-up comedian shouldn't do', giving a list of comedy conventions, some real, some imaginary. He then recited a list of 'what stand-up comedians should do' and gave exaggeratedly awkward responses to them. On various occasions he has also read out lists of things that will not be in the show, thus telling the audience what to expect: mainly disappointment. Then he provides a graph illustrating how the show progresses.

Ed started performing live comedy because 'I needed something to do in the evening because I was bored at work, so I did the course at the Amused Moose [London comedy club] and started doing stand-up'. He then managed to get on Jimmy Carr's *Comedy Idol* on British TV and won. It was the fourth time he had performed. Before he started performing he hadn't been to see comedy for ten years. 'It wasn't on my radar. My radar is office life. That's where my natural home is.' And indeed his performances often come across like an absurd orientation session in a bad office somewhere, with whiteboard and flip charts.

Aczel is deconstructing stand-up, taking it apart, showing how it actually works and exposing some of its lame conventions (including, admittedly, some advocated in this book). Aczel presents a scruffy, bewildered figure, inarticulate and almost wilfully shambolic. 'It's the Tommy Cooper approach: this is disastrous but nevertheless it is the show.' It is also very funny. He says, 'People put a grand title on it as being anti-comedy but it's meant to be a mess. I also never wanted to be particularly conventional. There were so many odd comedians in the 1980s and that's all I wanted to be: an odd comedian, someone who is trying something different.' Reactions have been varied and Ed Aczel tends to divide rooms. 'Some people love it, some people hate it. The distinguishing feature of my act is that there's no middle ground.' And he is happy with that.

Recap

If we have the will to perform and we feel we have something to say, there is nothing stopping us from performing live comedy. In fact, the more different we are from the usual single, white bloke, the better, as it gives us something different to talk about, a new angle that others may not have thought of yet. Man, woman, straight, gay, able-bodied or disabled, old or young – it doesn't matter. The important thing is to be what you feel is true to you.

We have looked at the basics of a comic persona here and noted that even the smallest details of style are important, such as the clothes we wear and the stage name we choose. However, the comedian need not be confined to presenting their own persona onstage. Comic ideas can be explored through an invented comic character and through different performance strategies. We shall look at these options in the following chapter.

5. The Comic Character and Others

When people think of live comedy they tend to imagine a solo performer with a microphone offering a string of gags, often autobiographical. But live comedy comes in many other guises. There are comic characters, drag acts, double acts, prop comics, magicians and ventriloquists, any of whom can bring diversity to a bill at a comedy club. Because they are different from the typical stand-up routine, these acts are likely to be memorable. In this chapter we will look at alternatives to the solo gag-*meister* and offer up a few possibilities to consider.

The important thing here is to use what you have got already, so if you can do a bit of ventriloquism or a few magic tricks, use them – if only briefly – so that your act stands out from the others on the night.

Comic characters

Whereas a comic persona is an identity based on the performer themself, incorporating their age, gender, sexuality or ethnic background as well as their personality and physical traits, a character is an invention. There are different reasons for performing as a comic character: because the comedian does not want to speak as him/herself; in order to satirise a certain type of person; or because the character can get away with saying things that the comedian would not say in real life.

When discussing the use of character in a stand-up context, the Brighton-based comedy teacher Jill Edwards has said the following (see overleaf):

You have to be careful with character acts because they can be the refuge for people who are scared of being themselves. I go for a very simple definition of stand-up: stand on stage, be yourself, tell people how you see the world. People confuse a monologue, which is acting and cuts out the audience, and stand-up, which is interacting with the audience.

This is not to say that comic characters do not work on stage but that the comic character needs to use the same approach as the persona-based stand-up comedian. As Jill Edwards says, it is not a monologue but a stand-up performance done in the guise of a character. For some people, being a comic character onstage creates a necessary distance of the 'real self' from the situation. The idea is that 'if the audience rejects the character, well, at least it wasn't directed at me'. A somewhat more positive argument for presenting a comic character is that you can present a microworld that is not necessarily your own and say things you might not be able to get away with as yourself.

The legendary American comedian Andy Kaufman made great play over the use of his comic characters, including his foul-mouthed lounge singer, Tony Clifton. Kaufman would use characters in a variety of hoaxes on comedy programmes like *Saturday Night Live* and was prepared to experiment and go way beyond the simple act of telling straight gags. (See the film *The Man in the Moon*, in which Jim Carrey plays Kaufman.) He would often confuse the audience as to whether the act was real or not, and his best work was closer to performance art than stand-up.

A more contemporary, though slightly similar, act is Neil Hamburger, played by American comedian Gregg Turkington. A classic example of the satire-based character, Hamburger is a decrepit entertainer, coughing and spluttering, wearing a tuxedo and plastered-down hairstyle, usually clutching a drink and making insulting jokes about various celebrities, among other things. As with Tony Clifton, some audience members are not sure if Hamburger is real or not.

The use of a comic character to satirise a recognisable social type can sometimes misfire. For example, the British comedian Al Murray's Pub Landlord character was intended to satirise the bigoted 'little Englander' type of person but was criticised by some people for unintentionally confirming those kinds of prejudice by saying what some of the audience actually felt. They took it at face value rather than as satire. Whatever the case, Murray's live DVDs show him at his best improvising, as if he merely needed to put on the costume in order to let fly.

Some comedians have several characters in their repertoire. The advantage here is that the performer can use different characters to suit different contexts. It stops the performer from being trapped in one character; however, hard work is required to make all the characters equally strong. We can see this potential difficulty in the case of British character comedian Steve Coogan, who created the Alan Partridge character for use on stage and screen. Although Coogan has also invented several other comic characters, few have been as detailed and successful as the dysfunctional, insensitive Partridge.

A comic character can easily coexist alongside a comedian's own persona. Expat American comedian Rich Hall has developed a curmudgeonly stand-up persona as well as the character Otis Lee Crenshaw, a country music crooner with a horrendous criminal record. Performing with a small backing band, this character has enabled Hall to explore the further reaches of humour, which his usual persona could not realistically touch upon. As well as being funny, the music was very well played (Hall is a serious country fan), and the act is made more memorable for it.

Building the comic character

When we invent a character we need to pose similar questions to those that we would if developing a comic persona: Who is this comic character and what is the point of presenting a character? Is it satire or something more whimsical? Unlike a persona, a comic character is a fictional one and requires some embellishments in order to work effectively: a costume, an accent and a back story.

Having a costume helps the performer get into character and adopt the mannerisms that accentuate the character's personality and indicate their social and economic status. Think of Charlie Chaplin's underdog tramp character, with his shabby, too-large black suit and umbrella, or the eponymous overall of Julie Walters's Mrs Overall. The costume saves time in helping to establish who the character is. This is an ancient trick in comedy and operates as a short cut for the audience, a sort of 'uniform' that will help them understand where the character comes from and what they are likely to do. For example, Neil Hamburger's greasy suit instantly identifies him as a failed and seedy nightclub entertainer.

An accent or voice that differs from the comedian's own helps to establish distance between the performer and the character. Al Murray's Pub Landlord has a strong cockney accent; Otis Lee Crenshaw's Texan growl is also distinctive; Neil Hamburger speaks with a grating, strained accent; and Dame Edna Everage has a high-pitched Australian accent which is instantly recognisable.

Caroline Aherne was in the BBC's *Fast Show* and wrote and acted in *The Royle Family* sitcom. She had previously invented a pensioner character called Mrs Merton who spoke with a strong Lancashire accent and hosted a chat show. During the programme Mrs Merton would recount various comic situations concerning her family, building up a back story that helped to make her character interesting as well as convincing.

The character's back story is comparable to the microworld of a comedian's persona. The more details that go into the back story, the more believable it is going to be and the more successful. The back story helps to build up a more complex identity to get the material over. Harry Hill's back story has considerably fleshed out his stage character over the years: we know that he has a nan, that his parents fed him chops and mash, and that he has had three girlfriends all called Jean. To take another example: Dame Edna Everage is married to Norm, who has a dicky prostate; she has a gay son and a much put-upon assistant called Madge Allsop. So although we know she is not a real woman this material gives her a quality of authenticity. All this is back story. It may be helpful when developing a comic character to write a short biography in order to establish who this person is and why they think and behave as they do.

Remember: the audience has to believe that the character is 'real', in the same way that we need to believe that the guy on the stage doing Hamlet *is* Hamlet, not just some geezer in tights. People really believed Andy Kaufman's characters and some also believed that Neil Hamburger was real. We can play with this, but the main thing is that we need to make sure that the character is convincing and that the material – what he/she says and does – is consistent with the character. To ensure this we need to observe how people like our character behave and talk. And the material itself should convey the person's background and how they came to this point in their lives.

Developing your comic character

Try doing the following exercise to help you flesh out your comic character.

- Write a biography.
- Get the costume right.
- How does your character speak?
- Perfect the accent and establish a personal vocabulary: Dame Edna calls everyone 'possums' while Mrs Merton used northern English colloquialisms that made her more authentic.
- What things bother them?
- What things do they like?
- Most of all, what is the reason behind presenting the character? Is it satire? Mockery? Or is it just an interesting or bizarre comic construction?

Man enough to be a woman?

A female impersonator is a man who dresses as a woman for either sexual or comic purposes. Whatever the reason it is always a performance – pretending to be someone else. In comedy there is a long tradition of female impersonation going way back to ancient Greek and Roman times and continuing to thrive in Shakespearean and other Elizabethan theatre, when women's roles were played by boys because it was illegal for women to perform onstage. By the nineteenth century this ban had long been lifted, but female impersonation continued in the form of the comic drag act. Developed by male comedians in British music hall and American vaudeville, these typically offered a grotesque parody of women – usually older women, disappointed with their husbands and the way their lives had turned out.

The tradition continued with various interpretations

through the twentieth century. Fanny Fairbottom was a British music hall act played by Norman Evans in the 1930s and 1940s; the Scottish comic actor Alastair Sim appeared as both a brother and sister in the film *The Belles of St Trinian's* (1954); and the *Monty Python* performers created some memorable shrill-voiced old women, from 'Hell's Grannies' to a couple of surprisingly erudite old biddies in a launderette discussing the work of the philosopher Jean Paul Sartre.

As the comedy and cabaret circuits have expanded, these transvestite characters now operate in fairly distinct categories, with the more sexualised performers on the gay cabaret and burlesque circuit and the more comical parodies, such as Dame Edna Everage, in the mainstream. It is obvious that these latter characterisations are men, an exaggerated version of 'how men think women are' and it is this that gets comic mileage: it is probably true to say that Dame Edna Everage has rarely been perceived as a 'real woman', rather than as a larger than life comic character played by a man. The British comedy sketch show *Little Britain* specialised in grotesque parodies, including an obviously male transvestite (with moustache) and some vomiting and urinating men-women.

Interestingly, drag need not be cross-gendered: the aforementioned British comedian Caroline Aherne's Mrs Merton character was as much a drag act as a parody of an older, Northern English woman, but one gifted with sharp wit when interviewing people. Given the chance, many comedy performers willingly don the dress of comedy at the drop of a wig. It seems that as long as it is grotesque and is not seen as intended to titillate, this is accepted by audiences.

However, it is the strong sub-history of female impersonators on the gay cabaret circuit that is worth looking at here. A good example is the UK drag queen Davina Sparkle. Brighton-based Davina Sparkle (aka David Pollikett) started performing in a gay pub in Hemel Hempstead, Hertfordshire, in 1996, having always wanted to do comedy and to dress up. Davina has sound advice for any man wishing to create a drag queen act: 'Always concentrate on your comedy and your show, decide what kind of act you are, e.g. modern, old style camp, etc., and learn your act, practise and practise in the mirror, *do not* go into it because you look good in a dress; lots of guys have great legs. And get someone to do your make-up. But this should be secondary to the show . . .' Davina has experienced few difficulties regarding sexuality when performing and makes a clear and important distinction between drag acts and other acts: 'Drag Queens are Guys in Frocks, we are not Lady Boys or Transvestites, we look glam but are obviously men. Most drag acts are gay, some are straight, but I really don't think it matters as long as you're good at what you do.'

Drag-act checklist

If you are going to do a drag act, whether it is a man as a woman, a woman as a different woman, or a woman as a man (all too rare), you need to apply the same principles as you would for any other comic character.

- The audience needs to understand the purpose of the act.
- The costume is a major consideration and has to complement the character.
- Pay attention to detail, whether autobiographical, make-up or clothing.
- Write a brief biography to help you develop a richer and more complex character.
- Most of all, what is the reason behind presenting the character? Is it for satirical purposes? Is it a mockery? Or is it just good old entertainment continuing a long and robust tradition?

Comedy 'foreigners'

As with cross-dressers, representations of 'foreigners' have a long tradition on the comedy stage and have been used for many different reasons. In the nineteenth and early twentieth centuries in America, white performers would often 'black up' and perform as comic minstrel characters in vaudeville, exaggerating for comic effect African-Americans' speech and appearance. This form of entertainment has now thankfully disappeared (although it was still popular in the BBC's *Black and White Minstrel Show* until the 1970s). In British stage comedy up until the late nineteenth century (and beyond), Dutch, French and Irish characters were often mocked; the frequency of representation was usually dependent on the relationship between that country and Britain at any one time. Comedy was used as propaganda either to send up 'fancy foreign ways', as in the classic French fop, or to present negative stereotypes such as the uneducated and drunken Irishman. Foreigners have long been mocked in jokes that people told among themelves, like the Polish jokes in the States or Irish jokes in Britain, which purposely stereotype 'alien' cultures and play on popular sentiments. Although such jokes have largely vanished from comedy circuits, some comedians have found other marginalised identities to disparage, such as disabled or gay people.

The stage foreigner needs to be a bit more complex than the comedy French cop Inspector Clouseau in the *Pink Panther* movies, and this is one of the reasons for their disappearance from live comedy: to be successful they need a *raison d'être*. One of the most successful comedy foreigners recently has been Sacha Baron Cohen's Kazakhstan character, Borat. Although this character has generated some controversy, Cohen's main aim in comedy, apart from making people laugh, is to expose people's prejudices, whether about race or sexuality. Borat performed in 'real life' and was accompanied by a film crew to record his various adventures among the unsuspecting. Of course, as with Cohen's other character Ali G, once people were wise to who he was, the game was up. However, Borat made a film of his adventures in America. One of its most memorable scenes – apart from the naked wrestling in a hotel room – entailed getting a bar full of people to sing his song 'Throw the Jew Down the Well'. This is a remarkable piece of film making, as Cohen easily gets the audience to give loud and lusty voice to a vile prejudice. Some people did not see the funny side, though, and the President of Kazakhstan complained that Borat was a prejudiced representation of his compatriots. That is his opinion. Other people saw Borat as a 'wise fool', adrift in a place he did not understand and not particularly negative; to them he was likeable and genuine, if a little naïve, and he exposed absurdities in both British and American life at the time.

A similar case occurred in the 1980s with British comedian Harry Enfield's character Stavros. This character was a North London-based Greek Cypriot who ran – what else? – a kebab stand. But rather than being a negative stereotype, Stavros was a very likeable and funny invention, to whom the nation warmed, and he usually got the better of those who tried to get one over on him. Although some critics objected to Enfield's stereotyping of an ethnic minority, the audience tended to like him and be on his side. He was never mean-spirited or malicious but just tried to fit in and get on with life, while offering a few insights into culture. Some of the laughter came from Stavros's malapropisms and Enfield's deliberate mangling of the English language, but in footage of the act the audience roar with approval and love to see him overcoming his difficulties. The problem is that by laughing at him, the audience may be worried about condoning racist attitudes. Certainly, characters of this sort have in the past been used for mockery, but we need to assess whether we are laughing *at* him or *with* him and, most importantly, whether or not he comes out on top of the situation. A racist joke denigrates someone because of their race and documents their social or physical differences. Both Borat and Stavros might be accused of doing that, but because they are likeable, complex characters they can be viewed in a more positive light. Borat and Stavros both undermined the audience's expectations and were 'winners'.

With a foreign character it is especially important to make sure that the character is believable and that the material is appropriate. We must also be aware that if it is a negative representation, some audience members will feel awkward about laughing at the character, so this possibility must be minimised by making the parody accurate and well rounded, rather than a lazy stereotype, which besides being unfair can become predictable and boring.

Getting your foreign character right

Detail is everything and like with any other character you have to make sure you get the accent and costume right and write a biography.

- Who is it?
- Consider their name – is it a joke one that sets them up for mockery? What does the name suggest?
- Where are they from? What is the back story and how have they arrived at this point in life?
- What is their relationship status?
- What do they do?
- What has happened that is significant in their lives to make them interesting and why should an audience be interested in them?
- Ask yourself: is it confirming prejudices or questioning them?

Double acts

So far we have looked mainly at solo performers, but there have been many comedy double acts who performed to great acclaim in both the UK and the United States: Laurel and Hardy, Abbott and Costello, the Muppets Bert and Ernie, Peter Cook and Dudley Moore, Morecambe and Wise, and The Mighty Boosh, to name but a few. Double acts work in many different ways.

One traditional form was the straight man–funny man combination. Crooner Bing Crosby and his comic sidekick, Bob Hope, made a series of popular movies entitled *The Road to . . .* (for example, Bali). Dean Martin and Jerry Lewis also made a successful stage and screen pairing, with Lewis as the clown (although Dino had also done his own sozzled comedy act at Frank Sinatra's Rat Pack gigs). Another successful double act, Dan Aykroyd and John Belushi, performed together on the seminal *Saturday Night Live* programme in the States and then went on to do their Blues Brothers film and tours. Gene Wilder and Richard Pryor made a couple of films that played up the straight white–hip black guy dynamic to comic effect. In some of his best films, writer-director-actor Kevin Smith appeared as the occasionally sagacious Silent Bob with his motor-mouthed partner, Jay.

In the UK, *Little Britain*'s Matt Lucas and David Walliams have performed a wide variety of unpleasant characters that have struck comedy gold; like Vic Reeves and Bob Mortimer, they eschew the usual straight man–funny man dichotomy. The Mighty Boosh have created stage shows that, like their TV and radio programmes, involve a complex microworld of talking gorillas, shamans, dance routines and dialogue – while still retaining the front-of-cloth comedy style of the traditional music hall.

Whom you choose to work with and the style you choose for your performance will be a unique combination of two separate personas related through a shared sense of humour. One advantage of being in a double act is quality control: there are two opinions about the material, so if one of them has any doubts about a gag, the chances are it should be either reworked or binned. As always, we need to be strict over what we think is worth performing.

Because there aren't many double acts on most live comedy nights, this kind of act has the advantage of offering a contrast with other stand-up routines. Even less common are comedy groups: three or more individuals performing together. We have only to think of the Marx Brothers, who went from the vaudeville stage to the screen with their style relatively intact. The logistics of group comedy can be complex – the stage has to be big enough to accommodate all of the members, as well as any props, additional costumes or musical instruments they may use, and most comedy stages are small and cramped. Space on the bill is another matter. The live comedy circuit does welcome comedy groups, as the League of Gentlemen have proved in Britain. The League won the Perrier Award at the Edinburgh Fringe in 1997 and went on to great success on TV.

Raymond and Mr Timpkins

The Raymond and Mr Timpkins Revue is an English prop- and music-driven double act. They have been around since 2004 and are as far away from the single male stand-up comedian as is possible. They started performing together in a spoof band in the 1980s and then went on to compère a local comedy club. However, Raymond says, 'We quickly became bored with watching white male stand-up after white male stand-up, week after week, and decided to perform something different to break up the monotony.' Inspired by Spike Milligan and *Monty Python*, they worked on the act for about five years before they felt confident that it had gelled. Music has always been an integral part of the act, as are props and costumes. 'Dressing up in outfits is customarily frowned upon in comedy,' notes Raymond, 'so it's always interesting starting every gig on the back foot and having to work to win an audience over.' When asked about the advantages of a double act, Raymond says they agree that the main one is never having to face the misery of 'dying' alone onstage. 'Stand-up can be a very lonely experience,' he adds, 'so always having a travel partner is a bonus, plus there's a great opportunity to develop an original dynamic as there are very few double acts working the circuit nowadays.' For anyone contemplating a comedy double act, they advise, the key things are having common ground, having plenty of stage time to experiment and develop the comic relationship but mainly being true to your own concept. 'It's very important to try to find and develop your own niche,' adds Raymond. 'Never rewrite to give an audience what you think they might want – always give them what you want them to have.'

If you are considering a double act, you and your chosen partner need to be compatible and understand what each of you wants to achieve. You also need to decide who does what in the act and how to solve any problem. Decide what your personal strengths and weaknesses are. Dialogue is crucial: at least one of you needs to be good at it. If you are both very good at it, great; but if you are both crap at it, find a new partner. Working together creatively will inevitably involve falling out occasionally over the suitability of material, but by adopting a code that says, 'If it ain't unanimous it ain't going in,' you can generally avoid future problems. Make sure you agree this in advance so that arguments can be sorted out and you don't waste time sitting in the pub being annoyed. Unanimous decisions are less likely to cause resentment.

Decide how you are going to write and who is going to write

what. Demarcation is important here; individual tasks should be allocated at the outset, so that no one encroaches on the other's territory, which might cause resentment. Look at each other's abilities; even those that do not seem intrinsically comic may be worked into the act. Juggling, music, impersonations and other skills can serve to kick-start comic interaction. Write down the dominant personality traits of the other person, write down what you think yours are, then read them out to each other and identify the aspects of persona that can be amplified and exploited. And remember that tiring journeys, falling-out with agents or management and failed gigs are much easier to cope with if there are two of you and the friendship is strong.

Prop comics

Like Raymond and Mr Timpkins, many solo comedians use props, which can be very useful for breaking up a string of one-liners and introducing a bit of variety into the act. They also help you stand out for the audience as different from others on the bill. However, only a few acts would describe themselves as 'prop-based comics'. George Egg is one of them. Well known on the UK comedy circuit, George started out performing as a street entertainer in London with a mix of 'magic, juggling, fire-eating and comedy' and has since performed all over Europe. He eventually started doing cabaret and the festival scene and finally 'drifted onto the comedy circuit'. He is quick to point out the differences with the various gigs, as audiences and expectations depend on the venue: 'What an audience accepts in a comedy club is not what parents with kids expect in Covent Garden [market].' George had to modify his language and subject matter when performing in the streets, and then when he decided to focus on the live comedy circuit he again had to readjust his act to suit expectations there. The act has always been 'prop-heavy', he says, 'but it became much more a "stand-up with props" show rather than a prop act with the occasional joke, as it was at the beginning'.

George has found little competition from other prop acts on the circuit: 'There's a surprising lack and I don't know why. It's certainly a branch of the comedy tree that has never been cool, so perhaps that's why.' And it isn't an easy option: 'It's also more difficult to sustain a prop act for longer than 30–40 minutes, as it is less chatty and involves fewer one-liners. A lot of acts use the circuit as a bit of a stepping stone to something more commercial and TV-based so a prop act which is just that, an act in its own right, is a less attractive option.' George says there are other spaces much more open than the stand-up circuit to prop-based comedy: 'There's a lot of prop acts and absurd acts on the cabaret circuit – performing at festivals and weirder, more off-the-wall nights around the country, but they're usually much shorter acts – five minutes or so, which isn't anything like as well paid [as the stand-up circuit], because there's more acts on, so there's going to be less money.'

Despite these drawbacks, a prop-based act is worth contemplating for several reasons. There are few competitors on the circuit; the act will stick in the audience's memory; it allows you a bit more creative freedom than simply shooting out gags; and the pace and style of the performance will also be different.

Improv classes for actors often use an exercise in which the performer has to create a monologue around a given object. This is a good way of generating material. Find an object, see what possibilities it offers, and then start to expand on it. One of my students had a coat hanger with a picture of Cliff Richard on it which he pulled out of a bag: 'Look, a Cliff hanger!' he said to applause. Simple but effective. Look at other prop acts to see how they use their props and gags and think about what kind of props are feasible on small stages: your elaborate finale with a full-scale guillotine may have to go. Also, the props must be hard-wearing – not likely to fall to pieces just before you go onstage or, worse, just before the punchline.

Building your act around a prop

Think about whether you can extend your act by adding one or more props.

- Can you invent or build props? If you have a gag can you illustrate it with something to build it up more?
- What everyday items could be incorporated into the act?

Magic!

As we noted for double acts, all sorts of skills, such as playing a musical instrument, can be exploited by a comedian on the live comedy stage. Magic, in particular, is a skill that can be used for great comic effect, as well as for its intrinsic fascination. Magic tricks can be anything from basic card tricks to more sophisticated sleight-of-hand manoeuvres and illusions involving complex contraptions. Joining your local Magic Circle and going to one of their auctions of props is a great way to meet people and pick up new tricks – and learn the patter that goes with it (used mainly to distract while the trick is being enacted). Pulling off a neat trick which is preceded by a few good gags and a bit of audience interaction can be greatly appreciated for its humour, skill and originality. Getting things (deliberately) wrong also makes for good comedy as this is a form of self-deprecation, and audiences love to see us fail.

People are naturally curious about how magic works and so there can be great play in this. Tommy Cooper made a career out of having a series of tricks go wrong and then somehow managing to perform one successfully. Penn and Teller were a fantastic magic double act (one very charismatic, the other totally silent) who made a career out of exposing how certain magic tricks work; they made compulsive viewing. Glaswegian comedian Gerry Sadowitz is a phenomenal magician and has incorporated various original tricks into his comedy act, as well as doing a straightforward (for him at least) close-up act with cards. The skilled magician can reduce an audience to kids by making us ask, how did he do that?

Ian Saville is a London-based magician who began performing when he was 11. His act is a mix of satire, conjuring and ventriloquism, originally inspired by Tommy Cooper, Woody Allen and Groucho Marx. As well as being in the tradition of political cabaret it also has connections to the old variety and vaudeville acts of the early twentieth century. Ian started performing magic when he was still at school and graduated to political theatre before combining the two and adding a generous dose of comedy: 'I suppose it took a year or so before I had an act that didn't vary all that much, but then I would slot in new sections, and by doing a series of Edinburgh shows based on the initial premise, I forced myself to create new material.' Although writing material depends on the idea of the actual trick, 'more often I muddle through a few performances, honing bits and adding new things as I go along.'

Ian's advice for anyone starting out with a comedy magic act is to 'concentrate on what you are interested in. Don't just do magic tricks off the shelf, but find ways in which you can use magic to express your view of the world, and your own particular brand of humour.' If you can do tricks, however basic, work out what kind of material can go with them and how this can be incorporated into an act. Work out a stage persona, whether shambolic, like Tommy Cooper; clever, like Penn and Teller; or unpredictable, like Sadowitz. Can you change the trick to make it funnier? (Sadowitz did a matchbox trick that featured a tiny penis.) Improvise with store-bought material, even if it is the most basic cup and ball routine, as there will be a gag in there somewhere. Remember that Tommy Cooper got a lot of comic mileage out of things going wrong, but when he did a successful trick he got a lot of laughter, even though it wasn't that funny. The placing of the successful trick in among unsuccessful ones was unexpected and the audience laughed out of surprise. Do your research: there are plenty of magic books out there; start by looking through them, because even the most rudimentary trick out of a book will mystify the average audience. And remember the folks at the back – they too must be able to see.

Ventriloquism and puppets

Ian Saville is a ventriloquist as well as a magician, and he notes the similarities between the two forms: in the so-called 'vent' act 'the puppet master operates the puppet in front of the audience, and challenges spectators to take note of how the illusion works'. Vent acts have been held up to some ridicule over the years, yet ventriloquism is a difficult but rewarding skill to have. Part of the problem was that the puppets were always a bit fearsome or the material was clichéd and weak. The old-school vents usually had a fairly scary red-cheeked wooden puppet (like Chucky from the film *Child's Play* but in tweed) which moved its mouth up and down while saying 'gottle of geer' or similar.

Although vent acts have understandably declined in popularity recently, there are some acts that bring a unique edge to the tradition and have revitalised it to some acclaim. In

2000, veteran British comedian Ken Campbell performed his one-man show 'The History of Comedy: Part One', which was based on reclaiming ventriloquism and putting it into a context outside variety, showing it as a historic art form that remains viable today. British vent act Nina Conti, who originally worked with Campbell, has performed all over the comedy world and is probably best known for her act with her simian companion, Monk. However, rather than restricting the act to the usual banter between person and puppet, Conti gradually deconstructs it, finally removing the puppet so that she ends up talking to her hand. Thus she exposes what the audience already knew but had suppressed: the monkey isn't real, it's a puppet, and the act is a clever trick. It is a strong finish to her set but also one that invites the audience to dismantle the illusion.

Traditional puppet acts usually try to hide the puppeteer – the classic example being the Punch and Judy shows, which conceal the operator in a small tent. Today, however, the puppeteer often makes only a half-hearted attempt at concealment, which enhances the comic effect. An example is 'Triumph, the Insult Comic Dog', the creation of Robert Smigel. Triumph usually 'smokes' a cigar, which repeatedly falls out of his mouth; Smigel can be seen putting it back in, thus dismantling any remaining illusion. Triumph relates his outrageous tales and generally insults the people with whom he is interacting. He has appeared regularly on Conan O'Brien's and Jay Leno's programmes, where Smigel can be seen behind a chair operating Triumph. He has something of a cult following.

Other stand-up acts have used vent dolls and puppets despite lacking any of the usual ventriloquist or puppeteer skills. For example, Harry Hill has incorporated ventriloquism into his act with different intentions: his long-term stage pal Stouffer is a blue rubber cat who sits in a little chair. Hill makes no attempt to disguise the fact that he cannot do the most important thing in ventriloquism – that is, speak without moving his lips. In his various TV shows, Hill has used ventriloquist puppets to retell the story of British pop band Take That. His act featured a vent dummy called 'Gary', the supposed head of Channel 4, who was desperate to appear in Hill's series. There was also a smaller cameo from 'Jonty', a string puppet who served no apparent purpose.

If we are going to do a vent act, we need to find an angle for it, as Conti has done with Monk and the deconstruction of the illusion. We need to get a puppet that we can work with, one that we can construct a personality for and start to build a relationship with. Although vent acts, being rare, will stick in the audience's memory, this is no substitute for the act being intrinsically a good one.

The fact that this 200-year-old tradition has waned in popularity suggests that it had grown stale and formulaic; so we need to bring something new to it in order to be successful. A striking example of vent innovation is provided by Paul Zerdin. Although Zerdin uses a variety of vent characters, he is especially noted for inventing the 'human ventriloquist dummy', which is both funny and original. Zerdin gets a volunteer up from the audience and fits him/her with a mask of a vent dummy's mouth, which he operates from behind. The hapless volunteer is then ventriloquised by Zerdin in a high-pitched, camp voice and then coerced into dancing. There is a tension created by how much Zerdin can push the 'dummy' and get away with it, and this can be played on to increase tension and get bigger laughs. He explains how he came up with the idea: 'I saw a ventriloquist do it with a man and a woman and he just squeezed the back of their necks and made them open their mouths. I thought, wouldn't it be fun if you had a mask and could control their every movement? And it is!' There is, he admits, a risk of the act going too far or the volunteer becoming angry: 'I had someone up once who was so drunk he could hardly stand. He took the mask off and threw it at me. That didn't go as well. But it was my fault, I should have known.' For anyone who wants to start a vent act, Zerdin has some terse advice: 'Try magic first, it's easier!' What we can learn from Zerdin is that we need to be careful about the choice of an audience volunteer but also that we need that unique angle, a dummy that is distinct from the many others who have gone before us and we need to look carefully at the relationship between vent and doll and try to find the right dynamic to make it a successful act.

Recap

We have seen that live comedy need not be simply a solo performer dispensing wisecracks. If we are going to do a character, we need to be as thorough as any other actor in researching the role, so as to communicate effectively with the audience. We can involve other things in our act, such as music, ventriloquism and magic, and we can work with partners, both real and fictional. The main thing is to choose the approach best suited to yourself. Do not do something because you saw someone else do it; but do something that comes naturally to you, that reflects your skills and interests and with which you feel confident.

6. The Performance

This chapter will look at how to structure a live comedy performance, from determining the suitability of the gig and preparing your material at home, to getting on and off the stage at the venue and finally leaving in a taxi – hopefully in a cloud of triumph. There are many potential pratfalls, however, which can easily be avoided by simply being prepared, and this preparation starts before you have even left the house. This chapter will look at the whole process of preparation, including how to overcome or at least minimise any problems you may encounter before or during the performance.

Getting a gig

The word 'gig' is used by writers, musicians, actors and even mercenaries all over the world, but for comedians it means any job or performance that they do at any venue with an audience. It is fairly easy to get gigs but you have to be prepared to travel and possibly end up out of pocket. If you live in or ncar a large city, getting gigs should not be a problem. If you live in a large town there will most likely be a suitable venue nearby; otherwise you will have to travel a bit. If you live in a small village, perhaps you should forget the whole thing and take up farming . . . Most venues will advertise in local or national newspapers and magazines, online and by flyers and posters dotted around other venues and bars. It takes only a bit of research to find a gig close to you, then pick up the phone and ask about getting a spot.

Most venues need performers and have an open-mic spot and so will be happy for you to come along and try out your material. Open spots are usually reserved for first-timers or those who have been at it for only a short while. When you ring up or, even better, call in, ask the promoter what kind of joint it is, who the audience tends to be and what kind of stuff goes down well. If the promoter says it's mostly strippers and the crowd love a bit of blue, forget it. Try to choose the right place for you and your material so you do not have to bend your material too much to accommodate an audience that you do not relate to. Booking yourself into an unsuitable place is almost guaranteeing that you will not come over well and this can set you back for weeks. Be sensible and be selective.

The larger the venue, the more unlikely it is that you will get a spot; even if you do, it is not a good idea to go straight in among the big boys and girls. The audience's expectation and experience are of a higher quality of comedy than you can provide at this stage and the other acts would be intimidating, which would not help your confidence. Start small. Find a place that is used by lesser-known comics or, even better, a place that has a night dedicated entirely to open-mic spots. These are usually midweek and are a good way for venue owners to make a little extra money on a quiet night. It is also ideal for you, as you will be among people who are just starting out and you can make contacts and find information on other suitable venues. You can also weigh up your material against theirs. Waiting to go on is nerve-racking, but afterwards, winding down with a beer, is an ideal time to chat, not only to other comedians but also to the organiser, to see if you can get another gig there.

The ideal comedy space should be enclosed, away from non-paying, non-interested customers and facing an audience who actually want to be there. The following two incidents prove the point. When I first started doing stand-up I was asked by a fellow student to come to a party in a nightclub and do my act. I was flattered. I got to the venue to find an uninterested audience who were there to dance; there was no stage, no lighting and a mic on a 60-centimetre (2-foot) cable leading to the DJ booth. I walked right out again. Later, still enthusiastic, I was booked to do an open-mic gig at a pub 'talent' night. I got there late to see a young girl singing *a cappella* 'I Will Always Love You' in front of a large group of very drunken lads screaming at her to take her top off. As I hurriedly left by the side door I heard my name being called repeatedly from the PA system, echoing down the silent street. I did the right thing. These two stories serve to illustrate a vital point: performing live comedy is hard enough, but there is no need to stick your head in the noose.

Once you have made sure that the gig is right for you and that the audience will be there to actually see some live comedy, you should familiarise yourself with the venue. It is often helpful to go there a week before and and check it out. Take a good look at the seating arrangements – where most of the audience will be and how wide the sightlines are. Seats are generally organised around the stage in a semicircle with the microphone as the focal point. The view from the stage needs to be able to take in most of the audience. There may be a pillar in the way or it may be an awkwardly shaped room, but you need to know the basic layout. Check out the lighting; in many clubs the lights are directly in front of the stage and are specifically there to blind comedians. Ideally you need to maintain eye contact with the audience so they know you are talking directly to them, but they do not know that often comedians can hardly see them. We need to create the illusion that we are speaking to each audience member individually.

If you cannot get to the venue the week before, at least get there early on the night. Again, walk around and familiarise yourself with the space, check out the microphone and stand situation, talk to the sound guy if possible, look at how much room you have to walk about in and how close the audience is, find out whether the microphone is noisy and how ferocious the lights are. These things will also help to lessen your anxiety and allow you to focus more on your set and the audience's response. If possible, get a friend to attend your first gig – someone who can later give you feedback on it. If they can take notes, so much the better. You may even be able to get permission for someone to record the gig, so that you can later analyse your performance and evaluate the audience's reactions.

In summary, knowing what venues to avoid is as important as knowing where to perform, so find the nearest and most suitable venue, ring them up and book a slot. Do not forget to ask what the audience and other acts are going to be like, as this will help when revising your material and tailoring your set. Either visit the place beforehand or get to the gig early on the night so you can familiarise yourself with it – you will be more at ease about the whole thing and feel as confident as you can at this stage about your set.

The mystique of timing

'What is the secret of comedy? Timing!' This is the conventional wisdom, which ignores material, persona and aptitude. But timing is important. It includes several different elements, which we shall examine here.

Rhythm

Ever since the time of the ancient Greeks, time and rhythm have been essential in comedy. In any joke there is a momentum that drives the joke along and must be maintained; the addition of an extra syllable – at least in a short gag – can bring even the most hilarious concept crashing down like a soggy tent on a drunken camper. We must not 'um' and 'ah' when we tell a joke and we must maintain its rhythm through the punchline.

Spontaneity

Another aspect of timing is the ability to respond quickly to an insult or slight. All of us have suffered petty humiliations in front of others and then thought of a response about an hour later, telling ourself, 'If only I'd thought of that at the time.' In the *Seinfeld* episode 'The Comeback', this is taken to ludicrous extremes: George tries to recreate a situation in which someone insulted him so that he can deliver the response he had thought of after the first time. Which naturally ends in disaster. The effortless delivery of a response to a pompous or slighting remark is the sign of a good comedian. This is why many comedians will not use prepared put-downs to a heckle, preferring instead to use a natural response. Spontaneity is important in live performance. Regarding the spontaneous put-down, if you can do it in the street, at work or in the pub, you should be able to do it from the stage. After all, you are a comedian.

Pacing the performance

There is also the rhythm of the overall performance to consider. The set must build up momentum as it goes along, through the use of increasingly complex material. For many comedians a set typically starts with a few short jokes, mainly to establish with the audience that they can do the job; then they get into slightly longer jokes with more elaborate set-ups, finishing with a climax, having maintained the tension to maximum effect before delivering the pay-off. This is timing in the sense of a gradual increase in pace.

Distributing the laughs

The timing of laughs is another consideration. Different jokes cause different amounts of laughter and the ones that get the biggest laughs need to be distributed carefully throughout the set. Obviously you should start and finish with the strongest, but you should also organise the rest carefully to give the audience variation.

The American absurdist comic Steven Wright has talked about organising his jokes into categories according to their relative strength, with 'A' jokes being stronger than 'B' jokes. The weaker jokes are interspersed with the stronger ones to vary the 'pitch' of the act: an A followed by a couple of B's then another A and so on. Audiences should not be laughed out halfway through the set by your giving them all A's at the start before moving into exclusively B territory. They need to be 'fed' jokes that elicit a range of responses, and this gives the set an overall rhythm.

Smooth talking

The final aspect of timing is taking your time when doing the gag. Do not speak too quickly or you may stumble over the words and thus throw out the timing of the gag, or the audience may miss hearing vital information. Hesitating and 'um'-ing and 'ah'-ing are also to be avoided. You should know your material and be able to perform it eloquently and with confidence. Nervous stumbling affects even the best jokes, and a good joke badly told is as good as a bad joke.

Organising the set

Once you have the date for your first performance you need to prepare what you are going to do on the night. You will already have a bunch of jokes, but they need to be put into some kind of order, called a set, so that the performance sounds professional and organised. A set is a sequence of gags that ideally move from subject to subject quite smoothly, starting off with shorter jokes to let the audience know that you are funny and to get to grips with your style, then moving on to longer jokes and finally to the closer: a strong joke or longer routine that builds up the momentum of the performance so that you finish with a big laugh.

Most open-mic spots last for five minutes, and for this length of set about a dozen one-liners or short gags and a longer closer are needed. We must accept that our material is variable and that we have some jokes that are stronger than others. It is useful to classify them into A's and B's as described above (if there are C's, don't use them, except to fill time, if necessary). An 'A' joke is one that you feel will work with most audiences. Of course, you won't be able to tell until you perform it, so if you can run through your material with a friend whose judgement you value, do this. If not, you have to trust your instincts and hope that if it is funny to you, it will be funny to others. 'B' jokes are the ones that are usable but not for opening or closing gags. These fit between 'A' gags in order to vary the amount and pace of laughter from the audience. Jokes build up tension in the audience, release it through the punchline then build it up gradually again.

Once you have organised your jokes into categories, look at each joke individually and ask yourself, 'Where does this joke work best in the set?' Play around with the order if you can. Do not start off with a rude or outrageous gag, even if it's one of your funniest. You need to get the audience to warm to you first by proving that you are funny, so do not freak them out. Instead, do another one of the funniest – but safer – 'A' gags, then move on to material that allows the audience to get where you are coming from, your angle, and the way you see the world. See if there are connections between two gags so that they can be run together. For example, if there is a gag about a train and one about an aeroplane, these can be linked into a longer section on travel by turning the two separate gags into a more coherent chunk of material, or 'bit'. A bit consists of two or more gags connected by a common theme, which move the act along seamlessly. Learn to identify connections and themes to create a professional and coherent performance.

Of course, not everyone wants to work like this, and a set of non-sequiturs or surreal, unrelated one-liners can be very effective. British comedian Tim Vine is a master of the one-liner and his gags have very little to do with each other. American comedian Steven Wright's material seems to occur to him at random.

You need to decide how you think the material will work best. If you have a bunch of one-liners, then pace them well and distribute them as A's and B's. If you have a set that flows from gag to gag, then stick with this, as it sounds professional and is satisfying to the audience.

Whether your gags are connected or disparate, the set should ideally lead from three or four one-liners into slightly longer gags, if possible dropping back into a couple more one-liners, then into the closer. Run through the set, rearranging the sequence if necessary, until you feel confident that it works. When you are happy with it, write down the order of the gags on a piece of paper – called a set list – and then stick to it.

In summary, open with your best one-liner which will establish to the audience that both you and the performance will be funny and thus remove any doubts they may have. Then as you move to the middle of the set gradually build up the length to a longer, more involved closer which is both strong and leaves the audience on a high note. This is the climax of the act which the other jokes build towards. We should always know from the outset how to finish and what impression we'd like to leave the audience with. After all, we want to be invited back.

The set list

Some people have retentive memories and can remember their lines easily (people with acting experience can remember a lot more lines than most comedians say in a night), but others are less fortunate. One of the major fears for comedians is forgetting their material onstage – drying up. This fear is not just for the novice comedian, as even the great and the good need prompting now and again. Fortunately there are ways to minimise this hazard.

Billy Connolly often performs onstage with a small stool on which a glass of water sits. His act is very rambling and he can segue from one subject to another in quite a short period of time. However sometimes he gets lost, and so he goes over to his glass of water and there underneath is a list of key words, which enables him to get back on track. Next time you watch a DVD or a comedian performing live, see if they have something written on the back of their hand or if they use a prompt like Connolly's. There is nothing wrong with this: it means you can deliver a better set for your audience. Which is the point after all.

The easiest way to write a set list is to reduce each gag down to a key word – for example, 'horses', 'betting shop', 'drunkenness'. Then you can do either of two things. The first is to write your list on a slip of paper, then when you get onstage put the list on a bar stool next to you with a drink (essential to stop your mouth from going dry and stumbling over a gag); after each gag, take a sip, check the list and continue. In the golden days when you could smoke onstage, lighting a cigarette or stubbing one out was also a good cover for list peeking.

The other option is to write the list on the side of your mic hand as small as possible and check it between gags. Try not to be too obvious unless it is part of the performance (at one gig a student of mine got a huge laugh simply by reading the bizarre things he had written on his hand to prompt him); otherwise you end up looking like a bad mime checking his watch – hopelessly amateur.

Given a degree of subtlety, it is better to use one of these safety mechanisms – as even some professional comedians do – than to freeze onstage and stammer, 'Er . . . I've forgotten what I was going to say.' But the best thing, of course, is to learn the material and remember it. The more you can organise your gags into coherent chunks or routines and the more times you perform the set, the better you will remember. As usual, practice is the key. It is difficult not to feel daft talking to yourself at home but stand-up is mainly a verbal art and your delivery can be improved by rehearsing in the same way an actor does. Away from others.

Doing the gig

So you have got your set organised, it's scribbled on your mic hand, and you're very nervous. Waiting around at a gig is often tedious, especially when you are so wound up you could explode. You will no doubt be anxious and start worrying over your material. Remember: you sat in a calm state of mind and worked it out previously. Do not start changing it now. If the material was funny before, it will be funny again. There is a temptation to play to your perceptions of the audience's prejudices and adapt the set to curry favour with them, but this sacrifices your original comedy voice, and you should have the confidence to stick to it. Be calm. Be confident. And be patient. Remember: you are also learning and trying stuff out and this is where you learn your craft.

Stage technique: meet Mic!

Nothing symbolises stand-up comedy more than the microphone beneath a single spotlight. But it also symbolises disaster for the novice who does not familiarise themself with this most important tool. One of the attractions of performing live comedy is its portability, the fact that we need very little equipment to do it (props aside). However, it does usually involve a microphone.

The microphone is a sensitive beast and it needs to be treated as such. Most smaller comedy clubs do not have an engineer to make sure there is no feedback or overload. Therefore the performer needs to know some basic rules to prevent this: as the mic needs to pick up your voice clearly it should be held about 15 centimetres (6 inches) directly in front of the mouth. Do not rest it on the chin or hold it down next to your chest. If you do not speak into the microphone, part of the joke may be lost and this will irritate the audience. Stand-up is lo-tech, but if you cannot deal with a simple mic it does not look or sound good.

Bear in mind that mics do vary, hence the desirability of testing the one at the venue in advance. But all mics are different. Look at how various comedians use their mics.

The way to deal with these irksome things is, first, to get onstage before the punters arrive. Take the mic out of the stand and test if the cable or lead is loose. If it is, the mic will make a noise when moved about and will distort or interrupt your voice. To prevent this, leave it in the stand and adjust the stand to the correct height. This may take a little trial and error. Mic stands come in many forms and all are specifically designed to annoy comedians. Make sure that the mic is fixed firmly in the stand and pointed towards your mouth at the right height so that it picks up everything you say. This has the advantage of leaving your hands free for props or gestures but also runs the risk of looking static; on a large stage a static comedian can look pretty lost. However, if the cable is not loose – and it usually is not – practise taking the mic out of the stand and holding it comfortably.

The microphone is connected by a long lead to an amplifier, which is a box that controls the volume and quality of the sound. The amplifier is connected to speakers situated around the room which distribute the sound evenly so that everyone can hear what is being said wherever they are in the room. This is a PA (public address) system, and in clubs they can vary from the excellent to the tragically ropey. They can be too feeble or way too powerful, with a very complicated mixing desk (which adjusts the sound quality) that no one seems to be able to operate.

Ask the sound guy, if there is one, or the organiser if you can go up and test the mic. This will give you an idea of how loud it is set. If you happen to be quite shouty, as many comedians are, this will distort the microphone and cause feedback. Feedback is the annoying screech that is created when a microphone overloads or the signal that has been sent out through the speakers is picked up again by the mic. This is most unpleasant. Gauge the volume for your voice and performing style.

Holding the mic, free of the stand, allows you to roam about the stage and also to move towards the audience and acknow-ledge their presence. However, if you do choose to wander about (which is also helpful in that it burns up a wee bit of nervous energy), don't forget to maintain eye contact with the audience.

Do not walk from side to side, displaying your magnificent profile, but keep looking around to make sure they are still with you. Time goes by *very quickly* up there, and it is essential to make sure the material is going over to the majority. It may just be your mates in the front row laughing and thus giving the illusion that the rest of the audience are onside. Check if those at the sides and back are laughing too.

Starting out with a mic

An exercise I do with my comedy students is to set up a microphone and stand onstage then line everyone up at the side. This can be intimidating but actually creates a useful sense of apprehension similar to that before any performance. The student comes onto the stage, introduces themself, tells one gag and then says goodbye. For a surprisingly simple exercise this throws up some interesting questions. Some pick up the microphone and speak confidently into it. Some cannot work out how to get it from the stand. Others bend down or crane their necks to speak into the mic. They have to make a split-second decision and then realise how important something as banal as this can be.

It is important to look comfortable and confident onstage, and ease with the mic will reassure your audience. Conversely, one giveaway of the inexperienced comedian is bad mic technique. When someone picks up the mic and says, 'Is this on?' or 'How do you get this thing out?' the audience become depressed to their very souls.

Props

Lord Baden-Powell, founder of the Boy Scouts and author of the unfortunately titled *Scouting for Boys*, chose as the Scouts' motto 'Be Prepared'. Like good little comedy scouts we need to be prepared for any eventuality, and this applies equally to props. If we are going to use props, we need to make sure they are near to hand – in a bag or a box or on a stool. A prop can be anything from a pint glass to a musical instrument or a ventriloquist's dummy and is something that is integral to the live performance. Even if the prop seems a bit cumbersome to drag halfway across town when it is only part of a single gag, if it guarantees a laugh you should use it.

In the days when smoking was allowed on stage, Geordie music hall comedian Bobby Brown used a cigarette as a prop. He would go on with a Woodbine (no filter) and take a drag after every joke, thus allowing the audience time to laugh and to maintain his casual approach (and get a nicotine hit). The cigarette was a timing device and when it was done he knew the set was over and it was time to go.

It is no longer possible to smoke onstage, even if it is a prop; however, it is a good idea instead to take a drink onstage with you (though not a triple vodka) for other reasons than to avoid comic amnesia. Taking a swig from the glass will give the audience time to laugh before your next joke; allow you to check a set list placed underneath it; or give you time to gather up for your next comic onslaught. A drink will also prevent your throat from drying up and affecting your delivery.

Before the show starts, put any props you need safely at the side of the stage, out of the way of other comedians so they don't get trampled but within easy reach for you to carry onstage as you go on. If you use a musical instrument, it should be tuned up (amplified if necessary) and ready to go. In my act I formerly used a David Hasselhof puppet (since stolen); made out of cardboard, it was foul-mouthed and spoke in a Geordie accent. This puppet would eventually be assaulted and apparently destroyed halfway through the act. It was kept face down on the floor slightly offstage so that the audience could not see it – which would have diminished the effect when it was revealed. I also use a banjo towards the end, which serves two purposes. One is that there are very few comedians who use a banjo in their acts, so people will remember it. The other is that the songs give a nice variety to the set before going into the closer. Banjos are also inherently comical.

Going on

Getting on and off the stage sounds like a relatively straight-forward endeavour (and for some it is) but it does need consideration. Let's start with the getting-on part. As always, the audience needs to know what sort of act to expect, and the way in which a comedian greets the audience can often influence how their persona is likely to be received. The MC or compère will introduce you (which we will get back to later in more detail), but you should remind the audience who you are (and also repeat your name on the way off). Make your introduction witty and pertinent: going on and saying, 'Hey! my name is X, so who's ready for fun?' may not be the most original approach, but it's a start. Making a comment about the venue, someone in the audience or the journey to the gig is a good way to start and lead into the first gag. However, do not be insulting to an audience member, undermine the MC or mock the previous acts, as it can be interpreted in the wrong spirit (unless the previous acts have offended the audience and you feel mockery is justified). Then get into the opening gag.

When Eddie Izzard started doing stand-up, his opening lines were usually a deliberately stuttered, mumbled waffle before he launched into his bizarre sequences. Norman Lovett (who played the original hologram Holly in the *Red Dwarf* series) presented a downbeat persona and opened his sets with long silences. Surrealist Brit Ross Noble's infectious enthusiasm indicates that his show is unlikely to feature a lot of overtly political material. Remember also that the name of the comedian can be indicative of their persona, so if someone introduces themself as Charlie Bucket we have an inkling that this character may be pretty zany.

Once you've introduced yourself, hit the audience with the first gag. If this works, the audience's confidence in the comedian is established and they will relax and trust you to be funny again. Continue to work smoothly through the set. Do not gabble. Just calm down and enjoy it. The major obstacle has been transcended!

Self-deprecation

I would do self-deprecation but I'm not very good at it. *Arnold Brown*

Once you have done the first gag and possibly made some remarks about the venue and audience, you need to show that you do not take yourself too seriously. This is a good time for the self-deprecation material. Self-deprecation is probably the first defence mechanism comedians develop. It indicates to the audience that, whether they are sitting in the cheap seats or have paid good money to see the performance, the comedian is really just like them, that he or she may be up there as the object of attention but has fatal flaws that will be revealed in the process of performance.

Initial self-deprecatory jokes are useful, too, because they can also pre-empt heckling: if you point out your own physical (or other) shortcomings, there is no need for hecklers to point them out. Jo Brand based a significant section of her early stand-up on deprecating her large size, knowing full well that she would otherwise at some point receive unflattering comments about it.

While dispelling any suggestion of arrogance on your part, self-deprecation paradoxically helps you to project a confident performance. It is all part of the live comedy illusion – of taking control of the situation by saying how unworthy you are actually to do it, and then doing it. Do not spend too long on this, however, as too much self-deprecation starts to become wearying. Endless fat/bald/lonely jokes tend to sound self-pitying and self-obsessed. Material needs to be universally appealing.

Succeeding at self-deprecation

Ask yourself the following questions:

- What is my most obvious physical characteristic?
- If I was going to heckle myself, what sort of thing would I shout?
- What aspect do I need to emphasise and how do I make that funny before anyone else picks up on it?

Confidence

We all know that a confidence trickster convinces their victim that they are genuine despite the fact they are not. Stand-up comedy is similar. For the novice comedian, standing onstage can be a frightening experience (and even disguising oneself as a character does not necessarily help). One golden rule is to *not* say, 'This is the first time I've done stand-up and I'm really nervous' to the audience. It will unnerve them and they will lose confidence in you.

Many comedians already have some stage experience from doing theatre at school, college or elsewhere. This can be very helpful – as you may feel more comfortable with the idea of performing and being scrutinised, and of using space and lighting – but stand-up is not acting. You are speaking directly to the audience. Performing live comedy is about control: you need to guide the audience into your microworld and entertain them there. You cannot do this if they detect nervousness on your part.

Although you may be almost catatonic with fear, try to *look* relaxed and casual. Make sure the first few jokes are easy to say – and for the audience to understand. Starting off with a verbally dexterous gag is risky: if done well, it may be impressive; if not, it will go wrong. If you miss a beat when telling a gag, this can wreck it. This is why one-liners are perfect here, as the chance of stumbling is minimised. Dispense them with confidence and the audience will be with you. The more they are with you, the less nervous you will be and the quicker you will begin to enjoy the performance. Once the audience have confidence in your ability, they will go anywhere with you. They will listen because they know the comedian is going to be funny again.

Should I stay or should I go?

After you've got the audience onside, you still need to keep monitoring their reactions. The relationship between the comedian and audience can be volatile, especially when still in the early stages; it continually changes. Ideally, they will go with you, but what if they do not? If this happens, get off. Unless you are contracted and paid to do a set amount of time, which is not the best idea for a first gig, you should cut and run. Do not try to convince them that they will enjoy your act; if they are not convinced in the first five minutes, they probably will not be after ten.

Overstaying your welcome backfires in two ways: first, it irritates the audience and turns them against you because they are *bored*; secondly, the room is affected negatively and this makes it tough for the next act to turn it around. (A good MC can remedy this, as we shall see later.) This is one of your first gigs and you're still learning your craft, so bow out gracefully. If the gig does go well, acknowledge the audience, say thank you and tell them that you have enjoyed yourself.

When I get my comedy students to perform for the first time I make sure the audience are going to be onside by putting the gig on in the university and getting other comedy students along who have been through it themselves. The students develop their act over five weeks before performing it. They are given constant feedback throughout, and on the night, if they are not going over well, a light is flashed to indicate they should get off. However, some students ignore this, fail to continually assess the gig and stay on too long, which is when the lights go off. Then the microphone. Then the security (me) forcefully ejects them from the venue.

When to walk!

Remember: there is nothing wrong with walking out of a gig if it is unsuitable. Although you may have been psyching yourself up all day for it and you will end up being disappointed, that is still much better than doing the gig, dying in front of an audience who could not care less and then walking home depressed, a scenario that can set you back considerably. You need to know when a battle is going to be lost. Especially if you aren't even getting paid for it.

The MC

A good compere is a bridge between the audience and the acts. He's a bit of both and a bit of neither. *Frank Skinner*[1]

When you get to the gig, introduce yourself to the MC and make sure they know your name and how you want to be introduced. Do not let them say something like 'Now here's a terrified young lad who's never done this before, please welcome Racist Tim!' This will not help.

The MC is of crucial importance: they are there to warm the crowd up, introduce the night and get the comedians on and off the stage. They are the go-between for the acts and the audience, available to smooth over the cracks if necessary and lessen any tensions that may arise as a result of sketchy performances.

Although the MC does act a part, the crucial aspects of the job are improvisation skills, a genial manner and an aura of control. If an act has fallen badly, the MC has to restore a good atmosphere – which is why they should be someone we want to see again, as a relief, if necessary. And if an act has done well, he should acknowledge it. The MC should be the sort of person you'd like to go for a drink with. They do not do a set but they bring in sure-fire bits from their own repertoire while talking to the audience and improvising in a good-natured way before introducing the next act. The MC should also know exactly when to come off. One danger of the job is the comedian's outsize ego, which drives us to hog the stage; but the MC must remember that they are not the act. They need to get the next one on.

Julian Hall, the comedy reviewer for the British *Independent* newspaper, says that a good MC is 'someone who can assert authority but within reason, is not bombastic or overly egotistical. Someone who allows the acts to do most of the talking. An MC should keep their contributions short and pithy, they are a thin layer of jam holding the bread together.'

Laughing Horse organise many comedy events in the UK and the opinion of their promoter, the comedian Bob Slayer, about what makes a good MC is well worth noting:

A good MC is someone who's got an interest in the whole show, not just an interest in themselves being funny – the show and the acts should come first if you are compere, and the compere (the most important act on the bill) is there to facilitate this and hold the whole thing together. There's a lot of skill needed as a compere – judging a room, when to do more or less after an act, bring the room up or down – even the ability to fill if an act hasn't got there on time. Generally knowing everything to do to make sure it's a good show. A good act doesn't necessarily make a good MC.

The MC, therefore, is a vital link between performer and audience, and it is a good idea to get acquainted with yours. If you are thinking about becoming an MC yourself, especially if you are going to run your own venue (more on this later), then watch how others do it, especially how they dovetail their rehearsed material with spontaneous banter with the audience.

There are performers who make great MCs and there are performers who make great comedy acts, and both of them are crucial to any comedy evening. If you think that your persona, style and material are suited to the role of MC, why not give it a go?

Getting off

After the closer – which should be an 'A' gag, memorable and strong (and if you must offend people, this is the time to do it) – the comedian needs to sign off appropriately. Remind the audience of your name and, if possible, attach a catchphrase to it: 'You've been great . . . I've been great . . . let's just forget this ever happened', for example. When leaving the stage the comedian should be tactful.

If the audience have been good (as they usually are), acknowledge it. If they have been difficult, slagging them off does nothing for anyone: it just leaves a bad taste in their mouths and an even sourer one in yours, which can remain for some time. We forget many of our performances, but the ones that end on bad notes unfortunately tend to remain with us a long time.

Off you go

Don't forget to say thank you, and make sure you mean it. Do not overstay your welcome. Once you have done your set, get off. Do not linger or improvise. Get off while they are still with you. Comedians who stay on too long are annoying. Know when to finish. Always. Go and get a drink. You have earned it.

A note on drinking

I got there at nine-thirty p.m. to be told I was going on at one-thirty a.m. . . . I ended up drinking about seven pints, so by the time I went on I was completely pissed . . . I came off traumatised, after five minutes, and didn't do it again for six months. *Arthur Smith*, on why you shouldn't drink too much before a gig[2]

Drinking can be an occupational hazard in the world of comedy. There is a lot of hanging around waiting to go on, the venues are often in bars and comedy business is often discussed over a pint or lunch in the pub. The false courage of alcohol is seen as a cure for nerves. It is not. There is nothing wrong with a pint or two while waiting to go on, but it is a poor substitute for good jokes and stage confidence.

The key thing to remember is to be more sober than the audience. They will no doubt have had a few drinks before the show is under way and several will feel loquacious and may want to join in. You need to keep your wits about you and, in case of heckling, be able to deploy a put-down with appropriate acidity and strength. In the grip of drink-fuelled annoyance, you may throw out a put-down that is way too strong, which is a good way of losing audience sympathy, however much you feel the heckler deserves it. As we've already noted, the comedian-audience relationship needs constant assessment, which requires a clear head (even though a lot of this is done subconsciously). For many people drinking decreases tolerance and increases confidence and aggression, so a bucketful of beer before going onstage may not be a comedian's best friend. There is no compulsion on the audience to be sober but they do expect to see a comedian in control of their faculties and their act. Sobriety is controlled and professional.

After the gig: did it go well?

So what have we learned now we are offstage? That performing live comedy is not easy and does take courage. Just remember, though, that your favourite comedian was once in *exactly* the same position as you: waiting to go on, uncertain and nervous, a martyr to the toilet bowl. Unless you chose the wrong venue – which means you weren't paying attention a few pages back – the audience wanted you to be funny and they wanted to hear what you had to say. No one was killed. You got up there, stuck to your material and did your best. You grabbed their attention and did the whole set. The audience were with you. Now, get on with it. Book your next gig as soon as you can.

If you were able to get a friend to come with you, they can give you feedback on what worked and what didn't. If they can make notes, so much the better. Listen to them, ask their advice and adjust your act if necessary. Do not forget the good feeling you got from doing well.

Did it not?

Despite being prepared, despite building up our courage and self-belief, it is inevitable that a comedian – even the best – will die onstage at some point. Performing live comedy can be the greatest feeling on earth, but going down badly can be very painful and we have to endure the bad with the good. If we understand why we have failed, this makes the failure easier to cope with. Everyone has bad nights. Not all audiences are generous and tolerant – sometimes you make mistakes. Everyone does.

Every comedian understands the risk of dying onstage. Dying is the complete rejection by the audience of the comedian's persona, style and material. The reasons may vary but the effect on a comedian is often the same: misery.

There are various reasons why an act does not go over:

• You were too nervous. So learn the material, learn to calm down and take your time.

• The material was not suitable. So make sure you research the next gig and that you know what the audience will tolerate and what they will not. (Even so, bear in mind that what works at that venue one night may not the next because all audiences are different.)

• The venue or gig was not suitable for you. So find others that are.

The misery varies in intensity according to how the comedian chooses to deal with it. The main thing to do is to try to see it in a positive light: we have to understand that it is part of the process of getting better, so we need to find out what we can learn from it. Rejection by the audience can be based on factors other than the comedian and their material. If this is your third or fourth gig, remind yourself that the act worked fine before, with other audiences. Thus a coping mechanism can begin to be assembled.

However, let us not delude ourselves: in many cases the problem lies with the comedian: weak material, poor articulation and/or failure to understand the audience's expectations. If that is the case, go back to the start of this chapter and work out where you went wrong. It may help to record the gig and listen back. (As it is your material, you are entitled to record it for personal use, to listen to afterwards.) Then you can identify your errors and the reasons for an audience not going along with you. Good comedy comes from hard work. The surrealist improviser Ross Noble is a good example here: he didn't just climb on stage and start improvising; it has taken years of hard work and focus to do what he does. As Oliver Double explains, 'Having started performing at the age of fifteen, he has been doing it now for almost half his life, and his improvisation seems effortless.'[3] For Steve Martin also, it took time: 'I did stand-up comedy for eighteen years. Ten of those years were spent learning, four years were spent refining, and four were spent in wild success.'[4]

And don't just take their word for it. For Lenny Bruce it meant: 'Four years of working in clubs – that's what really made it for me – every night: doing it, doing it, doing it, doing it, getting bored and doing it different ways, no pressure on you, and all the other comedians are drunken bums who don't show up. So I could try anything.'[5]

Believe in yourself, have courage, endure and weather the best and worst, but most of all be disciplined and professional.

'Is this funny?'

The only way to find out if something is funny or not – if it works – is to try it out in front of an audience. If a joke has worked before, it is funny. If it is rejected on a particular night, we have to admit that sometimes it does not work, but this does not mean we should drop it: we may just have chosen the wrong joke for that audience or that situation (who else was on the bill, what time you went on, etc.). If the comedian believes that the act works, based on the fact that it has worked before, then it can work again and we can endure. However, if each act is a consistent failure, there comes a point when endurance is futile: the act does not work because it has no comic worth.

As we've noted before, every comedian dies on stage at some point. It is part of the job. However, a cavalier approach to dying ('after the fiftieth time, one just gets used to it') needs to be discouraged for there is clearly a delusional aspect to this. No one likes being rejected, especially after working hard to create something designed to bring pleasure to others, but when an act fails repeatedly we need to consider why this has happened and then improve the act, getting rid of gags that are not working. It may be that only some restructuring is needed. For example, if the first five gags went well and the rest did not, then you could reorganize the set, spacing those five 'A' jokes at intervals among the rest of the material. But you should also be prepared to drop some material and write some more.

Discipline

Work really hard. If comedy is what you love then it's not like you're even working. *Hannah George*

If there is a secret to performing live comedy, it is surely discipline. And if you want to get anywhere in the comedy industry, where there is so much competition, you can gain an advantage through sheer hard work. The comedy industry is populous: comedy clubs are opening regularly; open-mic spots are increasing; more and more people are trying their hands at it. What makes the difference is how much time and effort you put into learning and improving your craft.

Performing live comedy is a way of communicating, a way of entertaining and a way of asserting our otherwise frail egos

over a bunch of no-marks in the audience. In this age of 'microwave' celebrity, when so-called stars are imposed on us after a small amount of TV irradiation, it is unusual to think of people actually working at their craft.

Unlike some other entertainers, comedians have to work hard if they are going to make it. No comedian has ever emerged fully formed, striding onto the stage to wild applause. For the vast majority of novice comedians, starting a career in comedy involves travelling to gigs that leave you out of pocket or playing to audiences who are waiting for their mates to come on or in venues that really should not be hosting stand-up comedy at all.

Recap

So now that the first gig is over and you are sitting at the bar basking in compliments with a drink in your hand, don't just rest on your laurels. You need to recap what you have learned here before looking at ways of improving your comedy and confidence in the run-up to your next undoubted triumph. Here is the checklist assuming you already have your very funny material:

• Find a venue and ring them, making sure it is suitable for you.
• Go to the venue you are booked to perform at, make notes about what kind of material is favoured by their audiences and talk to the other acts about the place. Treat it as a night out, but make notes in your notebook.
• Select a friend who has a similar sense of humour and who understands comedy from an audience's point of view – in other words, a comedy geek. Go through the jokes one by one and ask your friend if each joke is obscure, obvious or just not funny.
• Organise the set. Make sure it flows. Make sure you put the right material in the right place.

• Prepare. Get any props together. If you use a musical instrument then check that it is in working order and that you know the words to any songs.

• Streamline your set list. Get the material and trim off all the fat and padding. You may have five minutes but ninety seconds may just be unnecessary build-up. The audience will notice this. Make sure that the time spent in building up the gag is justified by the strength of the punchline.

• Also make sure that the words are easy to say – do not use words that will cause you to break the rhythm of the gag or long words you may mispronounce.

• Check that you have a greeting and/or a sign-off comment to begin and end the act.

• Do your research. Look at how your favourite comedians structure their sets, get on and offstage, hold the mic and start their routines.

If you are prepared and know this is the best you have, then there is nothing else you can do except learn it, stay straight and remember that if it was funny once, it will probably be funny again.

Nevertheless, you also need to keep the following in mind:

• Do not view the audience as the enemy, a cruel beast ready to massacre you. The audience want you to be good and will be supportive in the main.

• Do not use material that is 'all right' or 'okay'. The audience will only tolerate so much padding.

• Do not overwrite or overextend your jokes. They have their natural lifespan. Trim as much as possible to maximise the impact of the material. Better five minutes of good material than ten minutes that are okay.

• Learn your material.

• Forget self-consciousness as it only gets in the way.

• Believe in yourself. You will only get better.

If you are confident about your material and delivery style, if you are prepared, if you have left nothing to chance, then you should be fine. It just needs a bit of courage.

7. Jokes

Q: Do you have a favourite joke? A: No. *Lenny Bruce*[1]

When writing gags, I think you should use the least number of words. *Harry Hill* [2]

One good thing about getting divorced, it gave me about an hour's worth of material. *Lenny Bruce* [3]

Jokes are the essential tool of any comedian. If we want to perform live comedy we have to write jokes and this is tough. When starting out, the idea of writing a twenty-minute set – as professionals do – is intimidating, but this is possible with time, practice and discipline.

Many comedians start off by replicating the things that make their friends laugh, so we need to find out if what is funny to our friends is funny to other people as well. Or get new friends. A conversation with friends in the pub is funny in context and will have personal references that other people would not recognise. So if you got a laugh in the pub telling a story about your big night out, it can probably be transferred onstage, except that you will have to make sure you describe the people in the joke (in as few words as possible). Likewise, if your friends laughed at your account of being dumped, it is likely that others will too, as this is a universally recognised disaster zone. It is not hard to restructure the stories to weed out any obscure or specialised references. You were there, after all, and know what the punchline was. This kind of material has to make its own individual sense but it should still be about you and the things you know about. It is difficult to gauge what other people will find funny (or not) because what we ourselves find funny is totally subjective, but if the joke got a laugh once it should get a laugh again. The only way to find out if material will be funny is to test it out in a performance.

In this chapter we will look at all different kinds of jokes, from fast one-liners to longer, more complex routines. We will look at how to write jokes and what subjects to write about, and there are plenty of exercises throughout to develop your comic skills. It is just as important to know what *not* to write about, so we will look at what to avoid, the clichés and stereo-types that make dull and unoriginal comedy. We need to understand the current sensitivities on the comedy circuit to avoid making any gaffs that would alienate potential audiences. There is nothing wrong in principle with offending an audience, but you have to offend them with the right things in the right way! Finally there are a few tips on the skill of writing. But first, we will consider what a joke actually is.

What is a joke?

At its most basic a joke introduces a situation then builds it up to a conclusion that confounds the audience's expectations with the punchline. For example:

'My dog's got no nose.' (introduces situation)
'How does he smell?' (builds up situation)

'Awful.' (confounds situation through use of an extremely weak pun)

This joke should have been put to sleep by the comedy vet years ago but it serves as a good example: everyone knows what a dog is and everyone understands the two meanings of the word 'smell'.

The more recognisable the situation, the more we 'get' the joke, so a joke always needs a shared frame of reference for the comedian and audience. However, simply understanding the joke does not make it funnier: it is the imagination and originality of the build-up and the surprise of the punchline that make it stronger as a joke.

Some say that there are only seven kinds of joke in the world, but this is not the place to count them. What we can say is that jokes will always use several different devices to make their point, and if we can identify these we can use them to enhance our performances.

The English-speaking countries have developed a style of comedy that relies on verbal delivery (rather than more physical comedy, as in Japan, Italy or India) to wrong-foot the audience, and this is because of the profusion of synonyms in English. Just think of all the synonyms for 'penis' or 'breasts' or 'bottom' and you get the idea. This rich and complex language helps us to make jokes, and the would-be comedian would do well to think about this. We have words that sound like other words, like 'balls' and 'bawls', as well as single words that have two different meanings, as in 'The Secret Policeman's Ball'. The English language allows elaborate wordplay and is a creatively elastic medium. But that's enough linguistics, let's get on to something funny: comic one-liners.

The one-liner

The common language of live comedy is the one-liner, which introduces a situation, develops it and then follows it with a punchline that is logical but not (entirely) predictable. To reiterate: when we write a one-liner we need to select a familiar situation, an event that occurs there, and then confound our audience with the punchline. For example:

'A golf club walks into a bar [situation]

but the barman refuses to serve him [event]

"because you're driving later".' (a weak pun but justified by the brevity)

Many comedians have exploited the one-liner superbly. The American comedian Steven Wright has specialised in bizarre one-liners that are both original and hilarious. British comedian Jimmy Carr is a master of pungent one-liners, tailoring them to tease the audience's prejudices.

The call and response

The call-and-response joke is a short joke that usually follows the format of a question, as in 'What do you call a . . . ?' or, even worse, 'Knock, knock'. Although these gags can be used when performing live, we need to remember that they require an answer from an audience who may not be willing to get involved – in which case the question might just echo around a silent room, leaving you to answer it yourself. So if you have any call-and-response gags, try to rewrite them into a more singular joke. Rather than asking the audience 'What do you call a . . . ?' rewrite it into something that you can ask and then answer yourself so you will not be left hanging. At this unpredictable stage of live performance the novice comedian needs to avoid any possibility of error. If the joke must have a response from the audience but is too good to drop, wait until they are 100 per cent onside before you do it. Play it by ear.

Light bulb exercise

There are hundreds of light bulb jokes. Although they do not work as well onstage because we require the audience to respond appropriately (see below), they are great practice for the budding comedy writer. You do not have to ever use them live, but it is useful to save them in a file somewhere. Then, as you develop as a writer and performer, look back and see how much you have progressed. Although they have been done to death, they can be a good way of loosening up your comic imagination. Writing to order is difficult but it can be done. Try variations on the jokes below and opposite:

- How many comedians does it take to change a light bulb? Two. One to change the light bulb and one to steal it later.

- How many comedians does it take to change a light bulb? Two. One to change the light bulb and the other to claim they had thought of it earlier.
- How many comedians does it take to change a light bulb? Three. One to change the light bulb and two to reckon they could have done it better.

Your turn: How many students does it take to change a light bulb?

Puns and other wordplay

One of the most common language-based gags is the pun. In a pun one word or phrase is substituted for another that sounds similar. In Britain the pun is most often seen in the realm of commerce: a fish-and-chips shop called Jed's Plaice, for example. So a comedian might use this idea to invent a vasectomy clinic called It's a Snip or an adoption agency called Bastards. However, the pun is risky in live comedy, as jokes that rely on them can be predictable, weak or corny. With puns, the energy that is expended on the set-up always has to be justified by the effectiveness of the punchline. That is, if you are going to take a long time setting up the gag, the punchline had better be funny!

However, puns can be used effectively in the build-up to the punchline of a longer joke, rather than forming the punchline itself. In a longer anecdote about a disastrous holiday a pun can be dropped in to break up the preamble and keep the audience on track. Just be careful: if you use a corny pun you always need to highlight the fact that you know it is corny. Puns are not class A or even class B material, so acknowledge the fact, because the audience certainly will.

With puns and other wordplay there are subtle differences that we need to comprehend. Clever wordplay takes the pun up a notch. For example, Harry Hill did a gag about a stepladder – 'not my real ladder' – which is a clever play on 'stepbrother', etc. The following joke is similar to Hill's and depends on the phrase 'turn out' having two meanings:

'Did you hear about these new reversible jackets? I'm excited to see how they turn out.'

The next one is a pun where one word is replaced by a similar-sounding one but still maintains a comic logic:

'My neighbour's sprinkler is a constant irrigation to me.'

The words 'sprinkler' and 'irrigation' have a logical connection. But be aware that such simple forms of wordplay can be annoying unless they are particularly clever, and they should never be overdone. They are often merely amusing, rather than funny. British comedian Tim Vine does jokes that involve lots of clever wordplay, but he is also not embarrassed to point up a particularly groan-worthy pun. He intersperses these carefully into his stronger material. So long as you do not try to disguise inferior material as 'A' material, you can use it. A groan is often as good as a laugh and makes the set more varied and dynamic.

Similes and metaphors

A simile compares one thing with another of a different kind, using the word 'like' or 'as'. Closely resembling a simile is a metaphor, in which a word or phrase is applied to something that it is not literally applicable to; the words 'like' and 'as' are not used here.

Similes and metaphors are the comedian's friends and a cleverly worded one can get as good a laugh as a straight gag. In the 1970s the Scottish comedian Billy Connolly appeared on the BBC chat show *Parkinson*, which helped make his name.

On one occasion he observed, 'They made me feel about as welcome as a fart in a spacesuit.' This bizarre simile got a huge laugh.

Connolly's spacesuit simile works mainly because it describes an unwelcome situation from which there is no escape. The juxtaposition of a fart with an astronaut's life-support system is comic because of the element of surprise and the mental picture of the hapless trapped astronaut. With similes and metaphors, the more unexpected the comparison, the stronger the joke will be, so long as it maintains its comic logic.

Deconstruction

What we have been doing here is deconstructing jokes to understand how they work, but deconstruction itself can be part of your set. In deconstruction a comedian brings up a statement or subject and takes it apart in order to expose its inherent absurdity or meaninglessness. The Bolton comedian Peter Kay deconstructs phrases that people use every day and exposes them as meaningless, such as 'How is he in himself?'

The American comedian Louis CK did a routine that illustrates this perfectly: Louis relates how he had been driving badly and an irate motorist shouted at him, 'Suck a bag of dicks!' Louis explained the situation, which had actually happened and which many people who drive could relate to, then went through every possible permutation of the phrase 'suck a bag of dicks'. How many are in a bag? How long do I suck them for? What condition are they in? and so on. At the end of the routine he had explored all the different ways that this phrase could be interpreted and had come to the conclusion that it was essentially meaningless (although he got a lot of mileage out of it). This is what Scottish comedian Arnold Brown meant when he said that comedy has 'endless possibilities'.

Why is there no other word for euphemism?

We can see that when performing live comedy the comedian needs to use language creatively, rather than in an obvious way; the more imaginative the language, the more interesting and original the comedy becomes. One common use of creative language in comedy, as in everyday life, is the euphemism. A euphemism is a mild or less direct replacement word, most often used to disguise something rude or to disguise the 'grown-up' meaning of a statement. Examples of euphemisms include:

• 'I met Mary last night and she showed me her little lamb.'
• 'Apparently his parents are citing "musical differences".'

The first example is a euphemism for Mary's pubic area and there is still a comic logic to the statement because of the connection of Mary in the nursery rhyme and the play on the double meaning of 'little lamb'. 'Musical differences' is a mild euphemism for an acrimonious and often violent split between musicians but in this case it is applied to the hilarious world of divorce. In this example, which is a serious understatement, the meaning relies on the shared understanding and common usage of the term 'musical differences'.

When performing live comedy, the subjects of bodily functions, malfunctions and desires inevitably come up and it is here that euphemism can successfully be deployed. It is not hard to think of them, and in most cases, the meaning will be implied by the context in which it is used. 'Little lamb' is not a common term for a woman's pubic area but when used in connection with 'Mary', the implication becomes clear. The audience are forced to decipher the meaning of the euphemism and thus become a crucial part of the performance. There are endless euphemisms which stretch the imagination and can be used for live comedy. Here are a couple of the more bizarre ones from the wonderful *Wordsworth Book of Euphemism* – see if you can work them out: 'shake the dew off the lily', 'the Solicitor General', 'the exhaust pipe'. Menstruation is another topic offering plenty of scope for metaphor. Jo Brand once referred to it as 'Arsenal . . . playing at home'. (She also referred to female masturbation as 'gusset typing'.)

Rhyming slang is also euphemistic and the meaning is suggested by the rhyming of the last syllable or couple of syllables: 'Hampton Wick', 'cats and kitties' and 'John Hunts' are all fairly obvious and common examples. Although a lot of rhyming slang has come from either the cockney or criminal classes and is used by many people every day, as comedians we can use it in our descriptions to give more 'local colour' to our gags. Once again, the inventiveness of the rhyme gives our comedy a richer sound.

A note on sayability and rhythm

Remember that writing comedy is a craft, and good comedy craftsmanship entails writing jokes that are effective and easy to say. Pulling off a tricky tongue-twister may be audacious onstage, but there is always the risk of its going awry, sabotaging your air of confidence. Sometimes words that look good on paper are less so when spoken; this is especially true of puns. There is a difference between comedy written for reading and comedy written for speaking; good screenwriters know the difference and so should comedians. Best not to attempt poetry – stick to simple speech.

Of course stand-up comedy does have something in common with poetic drama: rhythm. Ancient Greek comedy and its successors, including Shakespeare, relied for their effectiveness partly on adhering to a strict rhythm. In a different way, jokes also depend on rhythm to come across effectively; this is the reason why joke structures such as 'Why did the chicken . . .' and 'How many X's does it take to change a light bulb?' remain in use today – they have a nice musical rhythm. The simplest way to understand the importance of rhythm in jokes is in the negative: when we are telling a gag onstage we can feel the rhythm building up to a climax, and if, when we reach the punchline, we gabble or stumble over it, the gag falls flat. This is because the preceding words create a rhythm, the audience are carried along with the impetus and then that rhythm is suddenly broken or upset. We have all had experiences in everyday life when we have fallen at the last hurdle of the gag. Onstage, this is amplified tenfold. Rehearse and edit.

Building a routine

When you start out you should have enough gags for a five-minute open-mic set – about twelve to fifteen decent one-liners. When you're a bit more experienced, the next step is to connect individual gags and expand them into longer routines.

Can we identify two or more jokes that have a common theme? For example, let's take travel: can we contrive a sequence of gags on the various kinds of transport? Suppose we have a gag about booking online and a gag about the tiny toilets on airplanes, what can we put in between? Can we write a link that gets us from squinting over our laptops to crouching over a suction-powered toilet bowl? We can create a list about the subject and work from that: arriving at the airport at 5 a.m., queuing to be searched, trying to buy duty-free fags and booze first thing in the morning when feeling nauseous, obnoxious passengers, terrible food. There are possibilities of things going wrong: delays, angry passengers, forgetting passports and hilarious comedy foreigners. Frustration is also funny when described on stage and is something everyone can relate to – especially where airports are concerned.

We can start to build up the routine between the two original jokes, adding others in a chronological order to tell the story more completely. The routine moves from one gag to the next and this gives the set a coherent feel. There is nothing wrong with a sequence of unconnected one-liners, but if jokes form a routine they are easier to remember, the audience are carried along by the narrative and it sounds like you are talking in an entertaining manner rather than simply reciting gags. This is down to personal taste, but watch how other comedians do it and see how they build up routines from different jokes on the same subject.

The long and short of it

A good example of an act formed from a sequence of linked jokes is Ronnie Corbett's signature monologues. In the 1970s there was a BBC comedy show called *The Two Ronnies* (Barker and Corbett). Each week Ronnie Corbett would sit in a chair and start to tell a long rambling joke but be constantly sidetracked into other shorter jokes, which turned out to be better than the actual joke he was telling. The end joke was invariably corny and would not be worth bothering about if it had not been used as an excuse to stick in a lot of much better material. The main gag simply served as a framework for a longer routine. The point was the journey, not the destination. Corbett's chair-bound performance served as a masterclass in how to structure a routine from a series of shorter jokes, and it can also serve as a model for a comedy set.

When we start performing live comedy it is essential that the jokes are short so we can keep in control and involve the audience in the material as quickly as possible. We can work up to longer gags and monologues as our confidence as performers and writers increases. We need to deliver jokes efficiently and not stumble over long words or complex sentences because jokes have rhythm and when we miss a beat the joke is thrown out of kilter and the punchline is ruined. The shorter the gag, the less likely we are to stumble. When we write a gag we also need to read it aloud to see if it is rhythmically satisfying and sayable. Check for any extraneous words that can be cut: if it is not building up the image or amplifying the punchline, it is not needed.

Crafting your material

To summarise so far, remember these guidelines:

- The strength of the punchline has to justify the length of the gag.
- If we acknowledge that the joke we are about to tell is going to be groan-worthy, then we can get away with it.
- We can drop in weaker gags on the road to a better one.
- Words must build either the picture or the punchline. If they don't, edit them out.
- We can use a corny shaggy-dog story to frame a bunch of other material.

At the London Comedy School comedian Adam Bloom explained about his writing technique and why he did not write out individual gags in full. Once he had thought of an idea, he would try it out using different wording until he felt he had the right combination that flowed smoothly. Writing techniques differ from person to person and it is up to the comedian how they go about it. If we write down the key points of an event (a tedious wedding, a boring journey) then improvise around the key points in our heads, we can build up the routine that way. If we know the set-up and we know the punchline, we have a more flexible bit of material. We just have to follow the chronological events of the day. So long as we remember the sequence and the punchlines, it should work out ok. When we relate a disastrous holiday experience to our friends we do not have a list, but we improvise round the various points, and we can replicate this for the stage. This kind of longer routine is great to finish with – it gives a climax to the set. A variation in rhythm gives the set a dynamic.

Reincorporation or callbacks

One of Harry Hill's techniques is the use of reincorporation, or the callback: referring to something he made a joke about earlier. He will bring up a subject on which he has several gags, such as shoe repair shops, do one or two and then move on to another topic. Every now and again, he will drop in another gag about the shoe repair shop, usually after an unrelated gag, so the audience suddenly click that he is continuing a joke he started several minutes ago. Reincorporation also makes the set feel more tightly organised. It is a clever and inclusive strategy which makes the audience feel more involved in the show because they have to work it out.

The way to do reincorporation is to select a subject and make a list of gags about it. For example, shops:

'You can't get a curry in Currys.'

'You can't get boots in Boots.'

'I couldn't find a house in British Home Stores.'

And so on.

Then, when writing out the set list, separate out the shop gags and intersperse one every couple of minutes – not so frequently that the audience are anticipating it but close enough for them to be able to remember the point you were originally making. When you have done all of the shop gags, tie it all off near the end with the punchline: 'But aren't there a lot of dicks in Dixon's?' The laughter does not come from the brilliance of the gag (obviously!) but by the fact that the audience are kept on their toes, realising and appreciating the cleverness of the set structure and the fact that the comedian has kept the joke going over a prolonged period of time.

Reiteration, reiteration, reiteration

Reincorporation relates to reiteration, which is saying the same thing more than once, either in exactly the same way or in a variation, to emphasise the point. Sometimes in conversation we can make a joke which gets a laugh, but when we try to add another punchline in order to perpetuate the laughter, the desired reaction does not always happen – mainly because everyday conversations are not supposed to be comic routines. A conversation should be a mutual two-way or multi-sided thing and the expectations are not those of an audience and performer. Also, the tension built by the run-up to the first laugh has dispersed and needs to be built up again rather than simply added to.

Although reiteration is not part of Jerry Seinfeld's usual stand-up routine, he emphasises this point in the *Seinfeld* episode 'The Burning' (series 9, episode 17). George is in a meeting where, for once, he actually makes a good suggestion, which earns him rare approval from his colleagues. However, he quickly squanders this goodwill with a weaker follow-through and is disconcerted. Later, when talking to Seinfeld in the coffee shop, he relates how he had them for a brief moment but then lost them. Jerry tells him that he has to leave them on a high note and refers to this as showmanship: 'When you hit that high note say goodnight and walk off.' (George, being George, proceeds to apply this principle inappropriately to other situations, with unfortunate

consequences.) Jerry's point is applicable when performing live comedy: the use of a double punchline does not automatically double the laughter unless the second punchline is stronger. It needs to be ordered properly.

If you have a gag with two punchlines, extend the part between the first and second punchline to build up the tension again. So, rather than one joke with two punchlines, make it one bit in two equal parts, each with a punchline. A comedian should always be looking to extend a gag into a longer routine which moves seamlessly from one part to the next and keeps the audience involved. Make sure you are not just saying the same thing twice. When you have two leads and two punchlines, put them in order, stronger one last. This creates a sense of climax.

Maximising the laughs with two punchlines

Remember: a laugh comes from the build-up and subsequent release of tension, so in order to get another laugh we need to rebuild the tension and take our time. There has to be a break between laughs and we must handle this carefully so that the audience can 'get its breath back'. Visualise it like this: build-up – punchline – build-on – punchline. Do not think: build-up – punchline, punchline. There needs to be time for the audience to catch up.

Observational comedy

Have you ever noticed that gags that start with 'have you ever noticed' aren't funny? Observational comedy is the comedy of everyday life and points out the inherent absurdities in the things we do or say. Dave Allen, Billy Connolly, Jerry Seinfeld and Tim Allen have all excelled at observational comedy. It is the comedy of recognition, which makes people say or think, 'Yeah, I do that' or 'I've noticed that'. It includes people in the shared microworld of the comedian and strengthens their relationship with the audience. Observational jokes look at things we did not know already or things we already knew but now see in a new way. Observational comedy provides for good 'story building' because of the repetition of visits to the bank or the hairdresser.

A lot of gags in this genre start with the phrase 'Have you ever noticed . . .?' Although this format tends to be a little overused, it can be a good way of generating material and developing a longer routine. The minutiae of everyday life are fascinating to us and our audience, whether concerned with mundane things like banking or more personal things like relationships.

This kind of observational comedy is directed from an outsider's viewpoint looking in on – as opposed to generating – the phenomena around us. We can all talk about traffic wardens or hairdressers, but what is our angle? What have we noticed about these people? What are we telling people that they don't know already? Can we amplify certain characteristics for comedy effect? Our angle might be to describe the traffic warden recruited from the SS or the aggressive hairdresser. What do traffic wardens and SS officers have in common? Uniforms, power and universal hatred. What do all hairdressers have in common? Strange smells, bad magazines and the intimacy of men (or women) playing with each other's hair. Can we present certain aspects and project a new version of something so universally recognised? As ever, there are dangers here, so always be careful of clichés. In some jokes, male hairdressers are seen as effeminate, so why not subvert this and turn the hairdresser into a psychotic, power-crazed hair vandal?

Jokes and tension have an intimate relationship. In everyday life we use jokes to dissolve tension. In awkward or tedious situations (job interviews, train delays, rows) a joke can dispel the tension that we feel. Often in a tense situation weaker jokes get a better response than they normally would get; the joke is playing on the tension already created and giving us a socially acceptable way of releasing it. Laughing when you are not supposed to (in school, when being told off at work, during sex) also increases tension and subsequently increases laughter. The more we try to suppress the urge to laugh, the more tense we become and the more we need to let it out. Laughter increases laughter.

No offence?

We can also create tension in comedy through the use of potentially 'offensive' material such as that performed by Sarah Silverman, Scottish stand-up Frankie Boyle or Jimmy Carr. The tension is created by the comedian talking about things we find taboo. We know that we should not find jokes about race or disability funny and we are aware that others see them as cruel, which creates a tension in us which is eventually released by the punchline. With this kind of 'offensive' comedy, there is also the fascination of seeing how far a comedian will go when pursuing a subject, and this similarly creates tension. With the likes of Silverman, Boyle or Carr there is an anticipation to see how appalling they can actually be.

Sometimes we can be surprised into laughter by the cleverness of a joke even though we may find the subject matter offensive. The laughter occurs before our moral censor starts operating: we laugh despite what we believe. However, this tends to be quite rare, as many offensive jokes signpost their offensive aspect fairly quickly – like racist jokes that start with 'A black feller walks into a bar'. We can 'prepare' ourselves to resist laughing, but sometimes we are caught out. As Ed Byrne says, 'Sometimes the wrong thing is funnier.'[4] A joke that says the wrong thing can surprise us into laughing anyway, whatever the subject.

Awkward comedy

With this kind of 'offensive comedy' the subject matter makes the audience feel awkward and thus tense. Comedy can also increase tension by putting the comedian into an awkward situation. Recently, there has been an increase in awkward comedy, personified by Larry David's *Curb Your Enthusiasm*, Ricky Gervais and Stephen Merchant's *The Office* and Louis CK's sitcom *Lucky Louie*. These comedies use an escalation of tension in a situation which increasingly gets out of control and becomes even more awkward. The more the character tries to get out of the situation, the more difficulties they get into. This awkwardness creates a physical tension in the audience which becomes almost unbearable. The tension is then released as laughter created by the outcome of the situation or the punchline of the joke. It is equivalent to blowing up a balloon until it bursts (bursting with laughter). This awkwardness is acted out in sitcom and described in live comedy, but both have the same effect on the audience – only with the latter we use our imaginations more to picture the situation. Ricky Gervais's stand-up is a good example of this. We could describe this kind of comedy as 'leave-the-room awkwardness', as it can become unbearable.

In live comedy we can use tension to our advantage by selecting a potentially difficult yet universally recognised situation – such as dating, which is full of uncertainty and has particular rules or etiquette that should be observed – and escalating the awkwardness. If it is something most of the audience members will have experienced, they relate to the feelings we are conveying as well as imagining themselves in the situation. The disastrous date is always a prolonged agony, full of potentially embarrassing behaviour. The first date also has comic potential because of the risk of personality clash, unsuitability, initial nervousness and uncertainty, the decision on where to go, the first or goodnight kiss, and the feeling of uselessness or rejection that these things usually entail. A dinner date is especially good material because both food and dating have rules and etiquette that ought to be observed, and the transgression of these familiar rules offers great potential for comedy. The greater the transgression, the funnier it is likely to be. The toilet is another area of potential awkwardness and this, combined with a date in a restaurant, has an even greater capacity for disaster. Noises, smells, upset stomachs, being overheard, being unable to go, the weird guy who hands you the towel are all ripe with embarrassment. The combination of the innate discomfort of the situation and the awkwardness of our actions compounds the comedy. This kind of thing is often used in 'gross-out' comedy films, and there are great examples in the films *Along Came Polly* and the *Meet the Parents* trilogy, all starring Ben Stiller. Stiller plays awkward characters who get into embarrassing situations, thus doubling the discomfort for the audience and racking up the tension. These examples rely for their comic effect on being over the top, rather than subtly escalating a potentially volatile situation. However gross, other people still will relate to it.

Exercise in discomfort

Take a universally recognised subject and move from a minor to a major disaster through a series of mishaps that escalate out of control and end in an absurd, embarrassing or unexpected situation. You have a dinner date and you are very hungry, you get to the place late, your date goes to the toilet then you drop a bread roll on the floor. You pick it up hoping no one saw and eat it but then realise your date has seen you. You are now caught in a situation that is going to escalate. What happens? How do you explain it? Then, in order to impress your date who is clearly unimpressed after such a bad start, you tell a lie about what you do for a living, get caught out and attempt to backtrack out of it. What do you tell them? What happens next? Think of it like a shooting script from a film going from disaster to disaster. Try writing out the sequence of events as bullet points:

- Reason for being late (bad stomach)
- Unsuitable date venue (place where you used to work)
- Pretend you do not know the other staff.
- Why were you fired?
- What are they like? Why are they unsuitable?
- What are you going to lie about?
- How do you extricate yourself from the whole situation?
- How does it all end? Badly, obviously.

Rules, possibilities and transgressions

Awkward comedy is based on rules or, more often, on breaking them, causing things to go wrong, which makes the audience feel tense and awkward. Even the punchline of a simple joke goes the wrong way. Think of slapstick comedy or jokes about relationships or politics. In their different ways, they all rely on things not going the way we expect them to. It is about surprise and this is what makes us laugh.

This kind of comedy is about our being involved in a situation, rather than being external observers, and it makes the material more personal. We have all made mistakes at least once in our lives, so we should be able to talk about these in a comic manner.

In everyday life we make mistakes when we ignore or do not know the rules – which is what Jerry Seinfeld and Larry David are particularly good at identifying. Wherever disaster can be identified and distorted, it can be turned into comedy. The audience will be genuinely curious about what happened when you transgressed the rules, as they either have been through a similar experience themselves or want to hear about someone else having such an experience. This is the voyeuristic nature of comedy.

Reality with a twist

Comedy is at its best when it is accurate and when the observations that we make are acute. By observing what normally goes on in a situation, we can then begin to twist it a little and use our imaginations to transform the everyday occurrences into something more bizarre, grotesque and funny. We need a situation where things can go wrong and then we can build on that.

Three exercises in distortion

These are everyday situations all with comic possibilities. Once we come up with the first joke about a situation there is always more to get out of it. We can then build it up into a routine.

- Everyone can recognise a coffee shop, where lots of completely different people are there for one reason: the consumption of overpriced caffeine-based beverages. Go and buy a cup of coffee and write down your observations about what you see. Look at the members of staff and the other customers – many people look like someone else, so who do they look like? Does the guy who collects the cups remind you of anyone in the serial killing profession? There is always a high turnover of staff at these places. Why? Is he killing them off? Use your imagination. Make your observations accurate.

- No matter where we go, there are always expected patterns of behaviour, so what about the supermarket? We only want to go in for a few items so what can possibly go wrong? What are the items and do they have embarrassment potential like a man buying tampons or a girl buying hundreds of condoms? Situate yourself in the shop and take a look around. The shop assistants are all expected to behave in a certain way so what happens when they don't? What happens when the deli man 'accidentally' puts his penis on the scales? Or the slicer? Who is in the queue and why have they not got their money ready? Are they paying by cheque? Are those discount coupons really necessary? What would you say to them if you could?

- Wherever there is food and drink there are manners and etiquettes that we all have to accept. What happens

when we transgress them? What is not acceptable behaviour in a restaurant? Have you ever had an embarrassingly posh dinner where you were trying to romance someone? Write down the key events like the impossible-to-decipher menu, the snotty waiters, the overpriced bill and the complete failure to impress the person you took.

Satire and topical humour

As long as there are politicians and famous people doing foolish things there will be satire. Writing satire or topical material is not hard to do. At work or with friends and family we often discuss what is in the paper or on the news and there are many possibilities to make jokes about this. Making jokes with our friends while watching TV is an adolescent pastime, but it can also be a good method of generating material. We respond naturally to the things we see, hear or read, and these can be the basis of a gag. For live comedy, as far as subject matter is concerned, we never have to look far for topical material; we can simply read the tabloids, watch idiotic celebrities on TV or listen to politicians to generate a wealth of good comic ideas.

In live comedy, freshness is essential and we need a frequent turnover of material to stop ourselves and our audience from finding our act too familiar. The comedian has to perform the material as if it had been freshly minted, despite the fact that it has taken a year to construct a tight twenty-minute set. When we do insert topical gags into the set, this reassures the audience that the material is relatively new and that we are clocking what is going on around us. It also confirms what many in the audience believe: that the tabloids are full of blather, celebrities are vain and vacuous and politicians are mendacious. This is the unifying force of comedy: when a comedian discusses something that we think is clearly wrong, it makes us feel that we are not the only ones to feel so. And although comedy can never directly change the world, it can reflect it and influence the way we think about things, and perhaps that is the start of making our world a better place. In America, some TV programmes, such as those of Conan O'Brien, Jay Leno and David Letterman, have used satirical or topical material, usually in their opening monologues. The animated programmes *The Simpsons*, *Family Guy* and *South Park* are also heavily satirical. In Britain, where audiences are more sceptical than Americans, satire has played an even greater part in the national sense of humour over the last fifty years or so: *Monty Python*, *Spitting Image*, *Have I Got News for You* and *Mock the Week* are held dear by British comedy audiences.

In the 1950s and 1960s, American satirist Mort Sahl used to come onstage with a newspaper and just 'talk' about the events of the day. This was a handy prompter and an even handier prop to play with for Mort, who had quite a nervous stage presence. Although to some extent this was a gimmick, the news was also a treasure trove for an astute comedian like Sahl: the words and actions of some public figures require little exaggeration to be ridiculous.

Although topical material is relatively easy to create, it also has a relatively short lifespan. We have to shelve really strong topical jokes once they have passed their sell-by date. A joke about the most recent Olympics may be an ideal closer for your set, but a few weeks after the Games are over, it will need to be scrapped. Or preserved for the next three and a half years until the next Olympics. Always keep gags in a file, even if they are no longer relevant, because they can be reworded and applied to new events.

Exercise in plundering the news

- Take photos from the newspaper and write captions to them as a kick-start for material. Can this be adapted into a purely verbal gag?
- Read the longer articles and see what stupid things famous people have said, then twist them.
- Pick on an inherently absurd event and expand on it. What happened? Why is it ridiculous? Can we use it to kick-start a fantasy? What would you do in the situation?
- Famous people are funny because they do things they should not do or try to ignore the rules that the rest of us have to follow. Think of all the jokes about Mel Gibson, Hugh Grant and Michael Jackson and you get an idea of the possibilities. They all made major transgressions and are therefore a great source for comedy.

Comedy and truth

Comedy should be true, in that it reflects the attitudes and opinions of the comic. *Frank Skinner*[5]

Comedy is often true. Not necessarily factually accurate but capable of giving us an insight into the world, an insight that we recognise as truthful – that is, likely. Observational comedy is particularly good at identifying things that we know to be true. Political material can also make us realise the painful facts of a situation. The skill of the comedian, whatever kind of comedy they are doing, lies in describing something truthfully as well as comedically. That is, they must talk about things from a point of view that audiences will find believable.

Of course, there are also many ways of presenting non-truths, which we should watch out for, and we will look at these next.

Cartoon world

In his book *Stand-Up! On Being a Comedian*, Oliver Double discusses the physical exaggeration used in many jokes, especially ready-made jokes that people tell in the pub. They exaggerate or distort physical characteristics – women with enormous breasts, men with large penises, blondes' alleged stupidity – and yet they do not provide us with an accurate picture of how something really is. These cartoons should be avoided, not because of 'political correctness' but simply because they are lazy and untrue and make for weak, dull comedy.

Clubs and traps

Jokes also create a sort of club consisting of the joke teller and the listeners. Typically, the club is created by a comedian sharing a joke about women with a group of men – for example, one about women being bad at parallel parking. The joke forms a 'men's club' that excludes women and confirms the men's negative ideas about them and the men's own superiority.

Although these jokes temporarily unite the men in their opinions, they fail to address the problems that men and women may experience between each other. The joke traps the situation, without explaining it or seeking to remedy it: it simply reinforces the negative ideas it contains. In this way jokes operate like viruses, spreading false information. Comedy always has the potential to speak truthfully about the world, and this lame and old form of comedy relies on the opposite.

Clichés

The clichéd woman takes ages to get ready, tidies things so that her husband cannot find them or is always nagging. The clichéd man goes down the pub too much, never changes his shirt and farts in bed. Do not do clichéd material.

There are a lot of comedians on the circuit and there is only a finite number of subjects to joke about, so it is important to try to find a new angle on these in order to create interesting and original comedy. Steven Wright looks at things in a unique way. So does Demetri Martin. What is it that makes them so different? They talk about things we all know but from a totally unique perspective. Watch them and study how they light up familiar subject matter in their own way.

Sexual relationships are universal, and because of this and because there is a body of conventional wisdom about what sort of sexual behaviour is typical, they have great comic potential. The danger is that the comedian will rely on clichés, such as farting in bed or the difference between men's and women's expectations. Try to focus on your own experience and observations.

This goes for other aspects of life also. Most comedy audience members are sophisticated people with strong critical faculties, have seen a lot of comedians and have had a wide range of experiences. Telling them something they know to be inaccurate or clichéd will get a cool reception. Choose targets carefully and truthfully, just as a good political cartoonist exaggerates a politician's flaws. Let's look at some universal institutions, such as families, school and work, that we can use because everyone knows them.

For various social and economic reasons, the mother-in-law joke is no longer a comedy currency. Until fairly recently the mother-in-law was a prominent figure in married men's lives because the young couple often lived with the bride's parents early in their marriage while they saved up for a house. Now, the social situation has changed and couples do not tend to live with their in-laws. Also, attitudes towards stereotyping have changed.

The British comedian Les Dawson was known for his reliance on mother-in-law gags; what made him different was his use of language, as well as the fact that he clung on to the form despite its being outdated. For Les it was not the content but the style that made him different: he had a superb vocabulary, so that although he stuck with the traditional mother-in-law gag, he brought his own style of expression to it.

A clever comedian can subvert a cliché. Lenny Bruce, one of the most original comedians of all time, subverted the mother-in-law joke perfectly – for example, 'My mother-in-law broke up my marriage – my wife came home and found us in bed together.' The typical clichéd mother-in-law is a domineering presence who vies with the husband for the wife's affection in a war between strong maternal attachment and the marital bond. In Lenny's gag, he plays on this stereotype then immediately swerves away from it by presenting a completely different image: that of the mother-in-law as a sexually attractive person and every bit as desirable, if not more so, than his wife.

Stereotypes

The most common kind of cliché in live comedy is the lazy stereotype. Certain jokes propagate stereotypes about other people's cultures or lifestyle choices, typical examples being racist and homophobic jokes. Although some people dislike these kinds of joke for how they misrepresent people, what is almost as offensive is that it is bad comedy. These jokes merely repeat ill-thought-out prejudices. Most cultures at some point

136

create a stereotyped figure on which to unload prejudice. According to Rob Long, a joke exploiting this prejudice 'takes as its premise the intellectual inferiority of a different and unsuspecting nationality'.[6]

The English used to deride the Irish, in an attempt to justify their own colonisation of Ireland (and how that has changed with the presence of so many interesting Irish comedians on the comedy circuit). Americans have used Polish people, among others, as the butt of jokes. And it seems everyone in Europe at some point has ridiculed the Jews (paradoxically, no one tells a Jewish joke better than a Jewish comedian). However, comedy has changed radically over the last thirty years and the social attitudes, including those of the audience, have shifted.

In Britain in the 1970s, the dominant jokes of stand-up comedians depended on unchallenged racial and sexual stereotypes, notably of black and Asian people and of women. The myths were used as an easy way of getting laughs. In 1979, a group of comedians got together at The Comedy Store in Soho, London, and began to devise a new approach to comedy. It was radical politically, fired by a post-punk energy and created by many people from fringe theatre groups whose grants were being cut by Margaret Thatcher's new Conservative government. This comedy challenged the old stereotypes, seeing them as outdated and irrelevant. The comedians wanted to talk about politics, pop culture, drugs, sex and relationships but in a way that was true and relevant to a younger audience, who were as immersed in pop culture as the comedians. Although this kind of 'alternative' comedy did not unseat Thatcher, it created shock waves in light entertainment, especially in TV, and woke people up to the shallowness of the old stereotype-based comedy. The new breed of comedians realised that comedy is at its best when it challenges preconceived ideas, when it starts from the bottom up, and that bad comedy relies on feeble thinking and attacks those in a weaker position than ourselves for easy laughs.

Archetypes

Whereas the stereotype reduces people to certain characteristics, the archetype tacitly acknowledges that we all have a lot more in common than we realise. There are things that most people do that are inherently absurd or comic and this is the unifying force of comedy. Rather than play on difference, it celebrates similarity. We can all recognise archetypical behaviour: kids are manic at weddings and funerals – and that is because they are bored; mums do tend to fuss over us – but that's because they care; and work is annoying – because most of us would rather be somewhere else.

It is true that a lot of blokes like football and they share certain traits: the only time they sing together is at a match; the only time they are tactile is in victory; and they can speak more passionately about their teams than they do about other things. These are archetypes. It also is true that many women could not care less about the offside rule, think football is a waste of good money and find football interesting only because some players are sexy. But not all men and women are like this, and exceptions can be found in your audience. If you talk about how women hate football and there are several women who go to see Arsenal every other week, then this will not ring true. Nor will assuming that all blokes enjoy watching overpaid jessies scampering around a wet field every week for ninety minutes. So think: does the joke reflect a comic truth – which is an archetype, what someone is likely to do – or is it a just a lazy stereotype? There are archetypical characters but also archetypical situations and we can use these in more observational comedy.

Old jokes and ready-mades

Today's comedians are self-managed and need to deal with the three principal disciplines of writing, performing and arranging their own gigs – all of which require work and dedication. If we want to be original comedians we need to speak in our own voice about the things that we know about from our own point of view. The use of autobiographical material and stuff we have written ourselves is essential here. There are many jokes that float through everyday life – called 'ready-mades' – that everyone can tell, but they speak in other people's voices. There is a debate between 'old-school' and newer comedians over the validity of using these jokes, which we will examine here.

It is not uncommon, on what journalists call a 'slow news day', for pundits in the media to debate the current standards in comedy and wonder whether 'the old jokes are the best'. The 'old jokes' tend to deal with the aforementioned outdated stereotypes and use comedy conventions that have long been jettisoned. However, it is fair to say that given the size of the comedy market today, there is ample room for all kinds of comedians and all types of jokes, including the 'old ones'. What separates the 'old-school' comedians, such as Bob Hope, Jack Benny and Morecambe and Wise, from more modern comedians is not just the subject matter, but also where the jokes come from. The principal differences are the degree of autobiography and the pop-cultural references, such as TV and other media, and drugs. Whereas comedians now write their own material, the more traditional comedians had scriptwriters.

Except for the improvisational element in their stage and TV work, British double act Morecambe and Wise used a writer called Eddie Braben. He knew the two comedians well and could write material to suit their different but complementary stage personas. Tony Hancock used two writers, called Galton and Simpson, who could write material to suit his pessimistic point of view. The comedians who were lower down in the comedy hierarchy had to pay by the joke or buy joke books via mail order and structure an act from those. Bernard Manning, who was known for his racist jokes and little else, built his act on 'ready-mades' that other people had told him. These old-school comedians were expected to perform, not write.

Since the days of Mort Sahl and Lenny Bruce, however, it has been understood that most comedians write their own material, which draws on their own experiences. Of course, there are exceptions, but on the live comedy circuit this is predominantly the case. The jokes that we write express our personal point of view and describe our own microworld; they have a stamp of authorship on them which maintains our comic voice. The difference between the ready-made and the more autobiographical joke is that the former is depersonalised; we get no information about the comedian and we do not really learn anything we didn't already know. Ready-mades tend to confirm an old idea of the world which most contemporary comedy audiences do not relate to.

Plagiarism?

There is a question over whether comedians should 'borrow' gags when starting out, whether gags can be adapted or even repeated verbatim (although everyone does it to a degree). The most difficult thing when starting out is finding the kind of things that fit the comedian's stage persona: does this joke suit the person telling it? Even some of the gags we write, although good, may not necessarily fit who we are onstage by being too strong or unlikely. Some gags fit right in there and cannot be done by anyone else – who else but Billy Connolly could do Billy Connolly? It is a slow process to understand our own world view and relate it to the audience, but for performers this is where the most honest comedy comes from: autobiography.

The most important thing for a comic, I think, is to 'find himself' onstage. To know who he is and why he is there. A comic, like I've said, needs to have a point of view. *Frank Skinner*[7]

The subject of plagiarism came up in one of my lectures. We were watching the previous week's stand-up performance on film and someone said that a student (who happened to be absent at the time) had stolen a gag from a well-known comedian. This sparked a debate, in the course of which someone pointed out that it was possible for someone accidentally to use other people's material without being aware of it. We do not know all the jokes currently in circulation and it is possible for two people to think of the same joke at the same time, especially with topical material that seems to present us with an obvious punchline. However, this is different from deliberate 'borrowing'.

There have been cases of comedians stealing other people's material, but this is to be avoided as much as possible as it is poor form. Material is the comedian's bread and butter and is often produced only through hard work. Nevertheless, even some of the best comedians have stolen stuff in the beginning. After a personal revelation Steve Martin realised that his material had to be self-generated:

This realization mortified me . . . I would have to drop some of my best one-liners, all pilfered from gag books and other people's routines. *Steve Martin*[8]

You have to start somewhere, of course, but not with other people's material.

The crucial point of view

One of the more popular kinds of ready-made joke is the Jewish joke. Jewish jokes fall into two basic categories, serving very different purposes. British comedian Bernard Manning told Jewish jokes, but the people in them were often negatively defined – for instance, they were cautious with money, and so merely confirmed the stereotype that 'all Jews are mean'.

In contrast, the legendary Jackie Mason, an ex-rabbi, talks about Jewish culture and tells classic Jewish jokes, but the characters he describes are canny and often come out on top of the situation. Not all of Mason's jokes are like this, but if he describes a negative attribute in Jewish culture it is from the position of an insider and is self-deprecatory. It is not an attack from the outside like Manning's material (although Manning himself had some Jewish ancestry). The reception of the joke, then, is determined by who is telling it and what their intentions are.

The same can be said for the 'N-word'. When racist comedians such as Bernard Manning used the word it was meant as an insult; by contrast, Chris Rock's superb 'Niggas vs. Black People' piece is an exercise in self-criticism. The intentions of Manning and Chris Rock here are completely different: Manning is being deliberately offensive towards black people, whereas Rock is being critical of African-Americans for conforming to stereotypical behaviour and is doing so from the point of view of an African-American. Rock urges people through this sequence to better themselves, whereas Manning used his offensiveness as a marketing tool, as without it he was merely old-fashioned and told tedious ready-mades. Manning used to justify his jokes by saying, 'It's just a joke,' and pointed out that he did a lot for charity. However, not everyone thinks virulent racism is 'just a joke'. Dealing with taboo subjects is fine but we need to make sure the audience is aware that we are criticising racism, not condoning it.

Racism is still *the* comedy taboo, and if someone is perceived as racist, their career may be a *Titanic*. Witness Michael Richards, who played Kramer in the American sitcom *Seinfeld* and who launched into a racist outburst onstage that pretty much finished his career for a while. Richards was doing stand-up at a club and was continually being distracted by some guys who kept talking despite his entreaties to them to stop. He then burst into a racist tirade which was recorded on a mobile phone and distributed round the Internet. You can practically hear his career crumbling as it goes on. After insulting the punters, he then tried to pass it off as merely a bit, which the audience did not go along with. Although many comedians must have understood his frustration, they would certainly have dealt more tactfully with the situation; insulting an audience member because of his race is professional suicide.

Shaggy dogs and rambles

The novice comedian, as we've noted, should stick to short, punchy jokes, which are easy to tell without stumbling and which will bring laughs at short intervals. But lengthier jokes can play a part in a set, once you get more experience.

The 'shaggy dog' joke has been a comedy basic for eons. It consists of a tedious preamble leading up to a corny pun or other silly punchline. The problem here is that the audience may feel that their time has not been well spent and that the length of the preamble is not justified by the strength of the punchline. This is the economics of comedy: the patience of the audience must be suitably rewarded. For many comedians the shaggy dog story has been justifiably put out of its misery long ago.

However, the shaggy dog joke should not be confused with the 'ramble': a long comic monologue studded with gags. Englishman Eddie Izzard, Irishman Dylan Moran and Scotsman Billy Connolly are excellent ramblers who can spin out long stories with enormous skill, tossing in great gags that sustain the audience's interest. The way of doing this is to have a broad subject about which you can make several jokes while getting to the point. The style of the comedian makes the ramble effective: Izzard specialises in surreal digressions; Moran at times seems apparently confused; and Connolly, who uses swear words very well, has an ability to swerve from one subject to another then go back to pick up the original thread. All these comedians rely on a lot of experience and a large backlog of material which they can draw on if they stray too far off the original subject. The way they relate apparently disconnected things to each other reflects their patterns of thought and their ability to see connections where others might not. Watch any of the above and see when the laughter comes. Most times it is not apparent that they are telling a gag because they have cleverly folded it into the main subject of the ramble.

The way to approach the ramble is to 'riff' on an idea: choose a subject that is ripe for comedy (and familiar to your audience) and improvise around its basic points. To facilitate this we can draw mind maps, corny though they may seem, as a way of identifying key points of the ramble. If we have just been to a funeral and want to convert this into material, how do we do it? (Nothing generates more laughter than other people's misery!) First, write down everything you remember from the day: the mood, weird relatives, any attendant disasters, attitudes towards the deceased, any controversy over the will, the job of the funeral director. Then, using the natural order of the day, write it all out as a list of key points and start to write gags for each key bit. Then write a few sentences about each and try to locate what was funny, or just odd, about them. We want to point out only what was funny that day. Anything 'poetic' or that does not either describe or create laughter should be edited out (if there is a secret to comedy, good editing is surely a contender). When we have a gag for each key point, we can rewrite the list of gags in chronological order and move from one to the other in sequence. The ramble is a great way to cut free of the more conventional joke while also developing your improvisational skills. It is a flexible use of material that will usually be different each time you do it.

What to joke about?

The surrealist British comedian Eddie Izzard once said that the most important thing a comedian needs is a good vocabulary, and this is hard to dispute. Having a wide variety of descriptive words to amplify the effect of the joke is always helpful. If we look at Anglo-fop Russell Brand's use of language, his verbal dandyism was what helped set him apart from other stand-up comedians. He successfully exploited his vocabulary as a comic device without making what he said too obscure. Jimmy Carr is also very articulate, which makes his oily persona all the more intriguing. So, once you've written a gag, see if you can rephrase it to make it more dynamic or interesting.

Words describe experiences, and these should be chosen in light of their potential audience appeal. On his *Pedantic and Whimsical* DVD, the Irish comedian Ed Byrne discussed what he had been doing over the previous six months – which was mainly travelling. He talked about all the places he had been and what he found of interest there, pointing out some of the local absurdities he had encountered. Not only is what he says funny and brilliantly described, it is also intrinsically interesting. The audience become involved in his stories because they genuinely want to know what his experiences were like. British comedian Phil Jupitus loves *Star Wars* and eventually structured an entire show (since lost) on the subject, which is something of a feat but clearly of interest only to those as obsessed with the film as he is. Byrne talks about a general subject (travel); Jupitus talks about a specialised subject (Ewoks and the like).

Although comedians have to be careful when talking about their special interests, for fear of boring the audience (the worst comedy crime), we can still talk about the reasons why some people are interested in a subject and focus on their idiosyncrasies. Trainspotting may be boring to some but there are reasons why people do it and the exploration of human motivations can make for good comedy. If you're keen on computer games or football, be sure to read the audience before going on. If there are lots of people wearing football shirts or spectacles, it's probably safe to get on to the soccer or PC game gags. If not, it's better to avoid them or find a new, more interesting angle.

Comedy has been around for a long time, but it is remarkable how little the subject matter changes. Ever since the ancient Greeks, comedy has dealt with universal human concerns: sex, relationships, politics, bodily functions . . . The details change with time and place, however, and it is the small differences that make for interesting observations.

The Greek philosopher Aristotle said that comedy should 'say the kind of thing that would happen'. He meant that although what we say may not be factual, given the circumstances it may well be true or believable. We have already stated that material needs to chime with the stage persona or character; even if this is clearly fictional, given the person describing it, it must ring true. Laurel and Hardy would obviously not survive most of their physical mishaps, but it is likely, given their characters, that they would become embroiled in such situations and so we accept it as true. Laurel and Hardy were also universally liked because they were gentle, relatively harmless and up against the things that people all over the world had to put up with. As was Charlie

Chaplin. Being silent, his movies could be understood by everyone, no matter what their language. It was the universal appeal of the little people against the world that created their success.

The universals in comedy are things that everyone can relate to: families, school, work, relationships and things like Christmas or birthdays. It is the required skill of the comedian to point out their particular experience in a unique way. We all have relationships but all are relationships are different.

The makings of a joke
- Think of the worst situation you have been in with a sexual partner and write about it.
- Think of the worst Christmas/birthday/wedding you ever experienced and find out why.

Weird families

Families are a universal comedy subject, but they are all very different, so your own family is a good place to start. Your parents, for example. Of course, all parents are mental, yet they are allowed to run families unsupervised while imposing their bizarre rules and habits on their children. You can probably find some comic material here. Parents always have catchphrases and habits, and when we compare them with our friends' families they become unusual and therefore ripe for comic exploitation. If there is nothing overtly unusual about your family (which I doubt) then exaggerate their mildly odd characteristics. Or make something up. Remember when you tried to sell your baby brother to the white slave trade or when your cousin ran a protection racket at kindergarten for sweets? There is an endless supply of material here, and, because you know your family so well, you can improvise and build on the material. Families are weird and holidays are disastrous, therefore they are a good source of comedy. Describing a disastrous family outing will give a ready-built narrative structure to your live set.

Family matters

To analyse your family's comic potential, consider the following questions:

- What are your parents like?
- What was it like to go on holiday with them? When did you stop wanting to go on holiday with them and why? Where did you always go?
- Did your parent swear? When did they first swear in front of you and what did they say? Exaggerate it.
- How did they speak to one another? How did they speak to you and your siblings? Were they different? What was the sibling hierarchy and where were you in it?
- All families have idiosyncrasies so what makes yours different? What about your brothers and sisters? What did you used to squabble about? What was the meanest thing you ever did?

Anthropomorphism: pets and objects

Families often have pets and these too are a good universal subject to get into, as all pets will be different. Here the comedian can use anthropomorphism: the attribution of human thoughts to animals or inanimate objects and, in comedy, getting them to speak or act like humans. Many audience members will have pets and will relate to this kind of material. In his *Live in Concert* DVD, Richard Pryor introduces his audience to police dogs, neighbours' dogs and fornicating monkeys, giving them all human voices and their own personalities. Billy Connolly did a piece about antelopes (one called Betty), who were being stalked by leopards. In the early 1990s Eddie Izzard did a classic routine in which he described hearing his cats purring behind the sofa. He then revealed that they were actually drilling for oil.

Bringing in your pets

Pets too can get in on the act! Ask yourself these questions:
- How do you talk to your own pets and what are they like?
- How can you invest them with human attributes?
- What does your pet think of you? What would it prefer to eat? What restaurant would it eat at? Or more likely, from whose bins?

We are surrounded by gadgets, which often break down, causing frustration. Most people have a fridge, microwave, toaster, mobile phone and so on, and these can all yield material for comedy. In the film *Swingers*, Jon Favreau has an answerphone with its own personality and he generates comic scenes from his interactions with it.

Talking to your toaster

Exploit the comic potential of all your gadgets by anthropomorphising them:
- Construct a conversation with your toaster on why it only pops up when it wants to, rather than when you do.

- What is the attitude of the toaster? Is it male or female? What are its voice and vocabulary like? Lazy? Authoritarian? What possible reasons are there for not popping up on demand?
- What about answerphones? Does yours deliberately screen your calls? Give you bad advice? Or act in a dominating manner to the people who call you?

School

Any collection of people who are brought together in a situation for a single reason will harbour the unusual, the deranged and the violent. This is as true of school as of any other situation. There are school archetypes such as the bully, the swot and the downright strange, but what made them all so different or frightening? There was the girl who got breasts first and made boys realise that life was about to get much more complicated; there was the one who always smelled of biscuits; and there was usually an incontinent or two. Teachers, too, are all different; and, as with any figure of authority who bosses us around, we have usually scrutinised and examined their quirks so can now turn them into comedy.

Like any other institution, a school has its own codes of conduct, with the inevitable transgressions of these codes – yet more good comic material. In any secondary school there is the simmering sense of sexuality, the uncontrollable hormones, the illicit act of smoking and the fact that many of us spent an extraordinary amount of time in the toilets: hiding, skiving or much worse. These too are rich sources of comic material. But watch out for clichés: sexy French teacher, boring maths guy, gingers.

Sex

Inevitably, in most comedy sets, the subject of sex will come
up, usually fairly quickly. There are two main ways of talking
about sex: the first is predicated on the idea that sex is 'dirty'
or 'naughty'. Many 'old-school' comedians seem able to talk of
nothing else and they become monomaniacs. The 'old-school'
joke discusses sex as if it is 'rude' and the laughter is generated
by the idea that it is wrong to discuss sex in public. This is a
very Victorian attitude. It is also an erroneous description of
the world of sex and of our own experiences, good and bad,
within it. If comedy is at its best when truthful, then
perpetuating sexual myths – such as sex is something that
happens *to* women and if a woman initiates sex she is a slut –
is the exact opposite: it is dishonest. Also, contemporary live
comedy audiences are more sophisticated and can tell you are
talking out of your arse.

The second way of dealing with sex and sexuality is to treat
it honestly, to describe one's own shortcomings (no, not those)
and experiences. Sex is funny in this way when we confess to

things going wrong or when it is discussed in a ridiculously exaggerated way. In the British sitcom *Campus*, the principal, in a faculty meeting, bombastically describes himself as 'swelling like a porpoise' the previous night 'whilst deep inside my wife!' It is funny because of the way he describes himself and also because he is completely unaware that it is an inappropriate subject for that situation.

As with the ritual of dating, sex makes for good comedy because it has its own rules and etiquette, and when these are transgressed the situation can become funny. There is a heightened sense of awkwardness in the sexual situation: taking your clothes off in front of a stranger seems weird, failing to please the other person is embarrassing, and ending up with an inappropriate and demanding partner can be frightening. Also, our bodies often do not respond in the way we wish them to, especially after having 'strong drink taken'; noises pop out unexpectedly, especially when in a compromising situation; and things either dry up or go to sleep when they should be doing the opposite. We all come to terms with sex and sexuality in our own awkward ways, and discussing our insecurities and outright failures can be part of the unifying force of comedy. When we constantly see images of perfect bodies and athletic sex in the media, we tend to feel insecure or uncertain about our own attributes. By sharing experiences, we show others that they are not alone in this and that we are all as awkward as each other at times.

By all means get on to the subject but remember two things: that sexual material, like scatological (poo) humour, should be in the middle or at the end of the set, after you have established a good relationship with the audience. Getting straight into the masturbation material is too much. The other thing to remember is that too much sex material gets tedious and you begin to sound repetitious. It is, after all, only one of many subjects for us to talk about.

Absurdity

A comedian needs an acute sense of the absurd. We need to identify and describe the ridiculous things around us in everyday life and explore them for comic possibilities. The question 'Why do we do that when we know it is wrong/ridiculous?' is an essential comic question. Much human behaviour appears absurd when looked at from a detached point of view. Look at the inherent absurdity of smoking. Smokers find pleasure in something that has the potential to kill us. Bill Hicks specialised in the smoker's black (-lunged) humour, exploring the absurdity of someone who recognises the danger of what he is doing – and then keeps doing it.

Such things as sport, fashion and drinking are all inherently absurd if we look at them objectively, and they have the added bonus of being universally familiar to audiences. Sport trains people to throw stuff far or run away quickly – both of which are transferable skills but not much use once we have left school. Fashion takes itself far too seriously: why are models paid so much for putting on a skirt? The fashion world is no stranger to camp behaviour either.

Drinking, like smoking, is supposed to be bad for us, but alcohol has the advantage over tobacco, from a comedian's point of view, as it makes us do very stupid things. It is unlikely that anyone has smoked ten Benson & Hedges and then as a result said, 'Let's get some coke and go to Paris!' Alcohol, like sex, takes a while to get used to, and our more ridiculous drink-fuelled exploits tend to occur when we are young and inexperienced. But not always. Some people never learn. Drinking too much is a universal experience, and many people can relate to that time you decided to paraglide naked from your bedroom window. Drinking is also a social activity and is as subject to rules and etiquette as any other. Transgressing these can make for effective comedy. The adverse effects of alcohol make our bodies do things that we would rather they didn't, and drinking can also involve various bodily functions, toilets, idiocy, sexual impropriety and a criminal record. All of which help make strong comedy.

Absurd habits

We can start closer to home and look at the ridiculous things we do:

- What about our eating habits?
- What don't we like and why?
- Why are we frightened by certain foods, such as tomatoes?
- Why are some people afraid of clown or buttons? (These fears are called coulrophobia and koumpounophobia.)
- Explain something you do frequently and identify its inherent absurdity.

The pointlessness of work

The reason why the TV sitcom *The Office* was successful is that work is a universal element of life for most people. We unfortunately have to work. This is why this classic British comedy has been adapted in the United States and Germany.

Increasingly, workplaces and jobs are similar, irrespective of where you are. *The Office* identified an area where people are in stasis: despite his loathing of the job Tim will never get out; Gareth is happy to stay; David Brent needs his position to shore up his idea of himself.

Work is a good subject for comedy for basically the same reason that school is: because people are forced to be there for a single purpose. People also identify themselves through the jobs they do. At parties we are often asked, 'What do you do?' Which means, 'How much money do you earn?' or 'Is it worth having babies with you?' Workplaces can be a menagerie of weirdness and thus offer rich pickings for the comedian. At work we often gang together with like-minded people to make jokes at the expense of co-workers and bosses. We can also be critical of the kind of work we are there to do, as it so often seems tedious and pointless. In any workplace there is the hierarchy of boss, middle management and the workforce, and where there is power there is usually a potential for humour; we make jokes about our 'superiors' as a way of redressing power or getting our own back.

Most of us have had several different jobs: summer jobs while still at school, part-time jobs, jobs we did while looking for something better. Jobs that we hated, jobs that exasperated us because they were so futile and dull. We may have had jobs where we were the only male/female there. All of this is good source material for comedians. We often resent these kinds of job, and the anger and bitterness they inspire are always a good launching pad for comedy. We get angry when we are frustrated and this can be funny to others. Situations where we spend an enormous amount of energy enraged about a trivial point can be comically justified: we look ridiculous when we are mad about something insignificant. However, we need to understand that over-focusing on something very trivial can also be boring, which, as we have noted, is comedy crime number one.

Looking at the workplace

To find potential humour in the workplace, think about your own jobs, past and present.
- What was the worst job you ever had? What was pointless about it?
- What were your colleagues like? What was the boss like?

What was the manager like?

- How did you get sacked?
- Who did you really hate? And was there someone you really hated for no proper reason?
- What about all the different people who work at the same level as you? What is wrong with them?
- Have you ever lied or exaggerated your importance in a company? What about euphemisms for lowly positions?

On the mood of writing

In a documentary on the satirist Peter Cook, ex-'Python' John Cleese said that whereas it took himself and his writing partner Graham Chapman two hours to generate two minutes of material, for Peter Cook it took two minutes. This is something most of us can only admire. For the rest of us mere comedy mortals, writing is a more difficult prospect. It is hard work and it takes time, discipline and a lot of trial and error. We also need imagination, dedication and perseverance and we need to understand that the more we write, the better we get. We need to accept that we can spend hours working on material that simply will not work when we perform it live – in which case we must admit our failure and move on. The test of any joke is: does it make people laugh? If it does not, bin it.

Any writer faces the issue of finding time to write. Putting time aside, or using spare time, as when on trains or buses, is essential. British comedian and TV presenter Frank Skinner once wrote: 'If I could spend thirty or forty hours a week drinking, I didn't see why I shouldn't spend fifteen hours a week writing gags.'[9] Unless you are surfing a serious deadline, fifteen hours a week may seem a wee bit excessive, but writing, like drinking, is a habit well worth cultivating. However, you have to know when and where. It is impossible to predict when amusing ideas will arrive but it is usually when you do not have a pen. Or at about 4 a.m., when you say overconfidently, 'I'll remember it, it's that good!' And then you don't. The average comedian probably throws away half a set a year through this kind of nighttime neglect, so keep a pen and paper handy at all times. Setting a specific time aside every week to write up notes may not be helpful, because writing anything is very much a mood thing and it is preferable to write when in the mood. Each person finds their own way of collecting ideas and turning them into jokes. Do not try to write when you are not in the mood, as it will lead to frustration and disappointment. Do it when you feel ready to assemble all the disconnected fragments scribbled in your notebook, on the back of cigarette packets and on napkins, and turn it into comedy gold.

The notebook

For this book I asked various comedians how and when they did their writing. Virtually all of them mentioned keeping a notebook (although the musical duo Raymond and Mr Timpkins also said that they use music to inspire them). Notebooks are the essential writer's tool and you need to keep one with you at all times. Whether it is a little pocketbook, a disposable 'reporter's notebook' with spiral binding that you can get from the newsagent, or something a wee bit more expensive like a Moleskine notebook, with its fine paper and pocket for scraps in the back, you need one. Whatever its form, it will have a value only you understand, as it is full of your ideas.

With the classic Moleskine notebooks, there is a space in the front for name and address and the promise of a reward on returning. You do not have to spend a tenner on a Moleskine to gain the privilege; your name and address in even the cheapest notebook can save a lot of heartbreak, as unformed jokes are harder to remember than complete ones. Veteran British comedian Bob Monkhouse lost two of his notebooks and offered a £10,000 reward for their return.

Without wishing to chastise Bob, surely he should have copied his notes up and maintained cheap, disposable pads as well as a better filing system. British comedian Zoe Lyons says, 'I scribble ideas down in a notebook.' German comedian Henning Wehn writes down ideas in his notebook and works up the ideas into routines, connecting thematically linked gags together when he has the inclination. Larry David uses an American notebook called the Boorum & Pease memo book, which features in *Curb Your Enthusiasm*, most prominently in the episode called 'The Wire' (Series 1.6) in which he misplaces it. It is interesting to see how pivotal the notebook is in creating a strand of an episode and how important it is to him. David jots down scenario ideas in his notebook and then, when he is ready, starts to connect them all up into a workable script. Losing the notebook can have disastrous consequences. If you carry a notebook it is essential to write up your notes on a regular basis; you do not want to lose it; but if you do, at least all the ideas are not lost. Keep on top of it, type up your ideas weekly if possible and make sure you have a back-up copy.

Laptop dancing

Do not let a pile of scribbles accumulate on your desk; keep on top of them, writing them up into your PC when you can. It is not unusual for writers to spend half an hour looking at a scrap of paper or a hastily jotted-down note that says something like 'Seagulls? Nazis? *Why not????*' and wondering what it is all supposed to mean. In the days of cheap laptops we can now create multiple files for our ideas: even if an idea seems unworkable, it is still worth writing it down and storing. Keep your files up to date; have a folder called 'Comedy' with a file for current gags, a file for gags that have been discarded, and an 'orphans' file in which to deposit interesting but as yet undeveloped ideas, because you never know when they may come back and be of use. British-Asian comedian Shazia Mirza says:

I sometimes sit at my computer and just write material, jokes. Other times I write down things that have happened to me, events and incidents, and then turn it into material. Or I think about things that I feel strongly about and think about what I'd like to say about those things. I'll chat to my friends about it and then write down our conversations.

All comedians use different methods to write, which depend to some extent on the structure of their routines. Connolly riffs on key points he has jotted down, for example, whereas Jimmy Carr works backwards from a punchline to develop his impeccably honed one-liners. Laurence Clarke tends to write 'late at night when there is no one around as I'm very easily distracted and can't stand the thought of missing out on anything. I tend to have an idea and think about it and develop it in my head for a while before writing anything down.' Mat Fraser takes quite a disciplined yet also somewhat 'rock and roll' approach and writes 'in the mornings. On my computer. Often feverishly. Then I go for a run or to the gym, come back and read it again, edit it.' For magician Ian Saville writing is optional: 'Sometimes I write a script, but more often I muddle through a few performances, honing bits and adding new things as I go along.'

Zoe Lyons says, 'Writing stand-up is a strange process for me. I battle with writing all the time. Some stuff can come out of simply sitting and writing and other stuff occurs when you are on stage performing.' Zoe also expresses concerns about her comedy orphans: 'You have an idea that seems hilarious so you jot down a few words. When you go back to it later the idea seems to have lost all its funny so you don't pursue the thought. Many a joke has died a premature death as a result of this lack of care.'

Comedian and writer Hannah George says, 'I write stand-up by accident. I find it very difficult to sit down and write a joke with a blank page, so I keep a notepad with me everywhere I go and if something happens or I have an idea for a gag/routine I will write it down and come to craft a joke out of it later.' Ed Aczel builds on the script he has performed previously so that his work has an organic development that grows and alters over a long period of time: 'Writing is much harder than anything else. I have a script and I just work on it. I start with last year's script and continue working on it until all of it's new and all of it's good. The rest gets cut. I keep copies of those scripts though.'

Aczel also works collaboratively: 'I have partners who I write with, I sit and talk with people about these things at endless dinners. I find it very, very difficult to endlessly write. If it was easy, there'd be more people doing it.' Paul Zerdin writes with others too: 'I write with a couple of people. I just think of an idea and then we thrash it out between us. Sometimes it takes weeks, sometimes months. It's a very painful process.'

Like performing in a double act, writing with a partner requires comic compatibility and a certain amount of diplomacy. The advantage of a writing partner is that we can discuss ideas and bring in new ways to approach subject matter as well as verifying if something is as funny to others as it is to us. It also means we can generate more material with a broader appeal than if we just focus on our own weird families, sex lives and hopeless obsessions.

Recap

To create good jokes, we need to examine why they work (or don't work). We need to avoid tired, racist and sexist stereotypes and focus instead on archetypes and on biographical material that is fresh and individual yet appealing to a wide audience. We need to find our own way of creating material, and this usually means writing. Whenever and however we write, the more we do it, the better we will be. One thing everyone acknowledges is that writing takes discipline and hard work. Being funny does not come easily.

8. The Audience

See, it's a weird thing, some performers are that naïve that they think there's such a thing as a good audience and a bad audience. A good audience would mean an audience that agrees with the comic's point of view. *Lenny Bruce* [1]

In his book *Stand-Up*, Oliver Double talks about early comedy recordings:

Instead of working to a live audience in a theatre, they had to perform their routines into a large metal horn . . . What really cripples the recording is the lack of audience reaction . . . the lack of audience laughs also makes the jokes inaudible to modern ears. [2]

Laughter is usually a communal experience. We generally laugh less when watching comedy on film or TV when on our own. Add one other person and the experience becomes a shared one. Add many others and we have 'the audience'. The audience is an enormous part of any live comedy performance and this is why it deserves a separate section: they have as much influence on the act as the comedian onstage performing it.

This chapter will look at the audience, how to get to know them, what we can expect from them, and how to tell the difference between a good audience and a bad one. We must know how to read a room so we can pitch the right material to them and we should know what to do to get them onside and keep them there. In particular we will look at the role of improvisation and how to deal with every comedian's nightmare: the heckler.

The performer-audience relationship

Live comedy audiences are not spectators: a spectator is like the cinema-goer, who has no influence over the order of events in the film. The audience for a live comedy performance can and do influence events. The performer-audience relationship is symbiotic: the one cannot exist without the other. It is also about power, and the balance of power can change quickly. The comedian must always keep a grip on things and stay in control. The audience is a bizarre and complex being: no one audience is the same; no one audience will react in the same, desired way; and no one audience can be judged too quickly, as they are so variable.

Where an audience is unified is in their purpose: they have all come out for a laugh. The audience's laughter indicates to the comedian that he or she can continue. If an audience does not go along, they can be transformed into a crowd and begin heckling. The point here is not to allow your audience to become a crowd, because although even the former can be a challenge, the latter can make things impossible.

For the comedian, any audience is a challenge which they should be able to meet, but we also need to remember that all audiences are different and subject to a great many variables. An audience's mood can be determined by where the venue is, what day and month it is, what the weather is like and how much people have had to drink. Student audiences are as different from Inner London audiences as New York audiences arc from L.A. ones.

There will always be gigs when the audience are not onside, are not interested and will not be swayed no matter how hard the comedian is working. Every comedian has their own horror stories of bad audiences. The stag or hen party can be a challenge, as they are not just there for the comedy but are a crowd in their own right. That is, they are not necessarily integrated with the rest of the audience and often have their own focus.

Some audiences have been known to be notoriously hostile, such as the legendary Malcolm Hardee's Tunnel Club in South London in the late 1980s. As Hardee wrote, the audience were 'referred to as the Glasgow Empire of the South: the audience at the Glasgow Empire hated southerners but at the Tunnel, they hated everyone.'[3] Tough crowd! But better that than no crowd? Maybe not.

It is perhaps not wise to dwell on the hostile audiences because they are not typical of gigs; but if you didn't do so well tonight, bear in mind an early Lee Evans gig where he was almost beaten up and had his car and piano stolen by angry punters screaming, 'Your f***ing life is shite!'[4] Perhaps Dominic Holland's words serve as more of a comfort: 'You have to remember that they're always there to have a laugh. They're not there to see you go badly . . . No one's thinking "I hope he stiffs".'[5]

As with many things, it is not size that is important but quality. An audience of twenty can be much more receptive than one of three hundred: it is the attitude of the audience and their willingness to be involved that can make or break a gig. As British comedian Frank Skinner says, 'Stand-up comedy is not a spectator sport, it's a participation event.'[6]

Sharing laughter is an intimate event, even among hundreds of people. For a good gig it is essential to get that connection – and you know when you have managed it and when you have failed.

Good and bad audiences

There are a number of possible reasons why the audience may not take to you and why it is not always your fault. They may just be a bad audience; they may be laughed out; your material may not be suitable; they may not relate to you. But what about when it *is* your fault? This is when you have to do something about the situation. You may fail because you appeared too nervous or you kept missing the beat of the joke. You may have misread the room and your material was either too strong (too sexual, say) or not strong enough (more scatology, please!). Or you may have come across as arrogant. If the material is not working, do not adopt the attitude 'This is great stuff and you have failed to appreciate it'. Arrogance is defensive, a front, and it alienates people. (Ironically, all stand-up comedy starts from a point of arrogance: the arrogance it takes to say, 'Listen to me, I'm funny'.) Again, this makes it harder for the comedians coming on after you. Which is not fair. We will come back to this presently.

Every audience is unique in its own right because the set is performed slightly differently every night to mainly different people. Some comedians offer their views on this. For Shazia Mirza it is very straightforward. When asked what defines a good gig, she says, 'Laughter'. And what defines a bad gig? 'No laughter.'

For the double act Raymond and Mr Timpkins there is a more subtle difference: 'A good gig can be a different experience to a good audience response. We always aim to be tight with perfect timing and no slip-ups – i.e. a good all-round performance which, hopefully, the audience buys into.'

For Zoe Lyons a good gig is where 'I am totally comfortable and on the ball and there is room to play. Where the "ad-lib god" drops a couple of beauties into your hands and the audience are up for it. Also it is not rocket science to set up a comedy room but when the room is set right it does go a long way to making a good gig.' A bad gig for Zoe would be 'performing to office Christmas parties'.

For Mat Fraser a good gig is when 'lots of people go and they love it. Bad is when they don't laugh, however many people are there, indeed the more people not laughing, the worse the gig is for me.'

For comedian and writer Hannah George it is simple: a good gig is 'full of laughs. Turning a bad crowd into a good one. Doing some brilliant improv. Thinking up heckler comebacks on the spot, not on the train home.' A bad one for Hannah is 'coming across as the wrong sort of person. It sounds odd, but if a couple of jokes go badly, or you don't feel as though you've set yourself up with your onstage persona then the jokes can really fall flat. The same goes for every other act really. If I don't set myself up as being quite sweet, then a lot of my material can just make me sound like a bitchy slag. And I save that for the toilets after the show.'

What most comedians can agree on is that most audiences are unpredictable and that you never know who is going to turn up and how it is going to turn out, however prepared you are. But every kind of preparation helps, including working out who your audience are.

Reading the room

Never underestimate the importance of reading the room. One of the many mistakes the novice comedian can make is not understanding the make-up of the audience, who it actually consists of and what kind of material they are likely to take to. One stand-up gig I organised serves as a classic example: a student came onstage and started off with a very disparaging joke about disabled kids on sports day. However, he had not checked out the room before he went on and had failed to see the severely disabled guy in the wheelchair in the middle of the front row. Result: sudden comedy death. The entire audience had clocked the guy coming in and tensed up immediately, and the set was lost. It took the MC a lot of work to bring it back up again and for the audience to forget the blunder. All it takes is a quick peep round the curtains or a stroll through the audience to avoid this.

Assessing the audience make-up is vital in order to maximise the impact of your material. If it is a student gig, then they will absorb some dodgy material that perhaps a wedding reception would baulk at. If it is a sporty lads' night, the soccer gags will work. If it's the hens, forget the soccer gags. The gender make-up of many comedy-club audiences is fairly even (although female acts make up only 10 per cent on the circuit) and it is important to understand what material will work for both sexes. On one occasion some of my comedy students came to my home town, Brighton, to help out at a benefit show which a friend had organised. One of the students, who had won a comedy award, was a lad whose material dealt mainly with his favourite soccer team and his sexual habits now that his girlfriend had left him. On the way home, a female friend said to me: 'I just don't need to know about Chelsea or an 18-year-old masturbating.' Fair point.

Comedy often deals with taboos and risqué subjects and this is what makes it fun and provocative. However, there is a time and place for all subjects to be used effectively, and reading the room can prevent the set from going over badly. Doing sick or even risqué material right off runs the risk of alienating your audience. You need to get the confidence of the audience first and then gradually get them involved in the more edgy material. Look at who the audience are and what kind of material you think they will accept. If they are young you can talk about certain things but if they are older then you have to make sure that your material will still appeal to them and not be too obscure.

A comedian's material needs to be appropriate for the person onstage saying it but we also need to identify anything that could be seen as offensive or controversial. As ever, walking through the audience, watching the other acts and what the audience do not respond to can save the day. Make any necessary amendments to guarantee your act will go over in the best possible way. Whatever you do, make sure the material does not embarrass, bore or alienate the audience.

Things to avoid

Three major things you should never do to an audience until you are totally in control of your act are to make them feel awkward, make them yawn or make them wonder what the hell you are going on about. Although there is a strong element of awkward comedy (performances by Larry David, Ben Stiller and Steve Coogan are just a few good examples) it is structured in a particular way for comic effect. The awkward situation is carefully escalated as it spins out of control, but then the tension in the audience is released with a well-placed punchline. This is comic skill. However, the embarrassed audience feel awkward, not because of comic skill, but by lack of it. An uncomfortable audience is reluctant to laugh, and nervous laughter is not the laughter we require. Get offstage if things have got so bad.

Remember!

As mentioned earlier, there is nothing wrong with walking offstage because the material is not working. At this stage you are not being paid for it, you will probably find it difficult getting the audience back onside and, if you do not, it will further damage your confidence, which you do not need right now. Remember also that the MC and subsequent acts are going to have to work harder to win the audience back again and make up for your mistakes. This is not fair on the MC, the other comedians and especially the audience. The longer you prolong the embarrassment, the longer it will take for the gig to recover – which you won't notice as you will be in the car park weeping with shame.

Boring the audience

The audience is a beast but one that needs feeding now and then, and there are several ways to send it to sleep. Longueurs – gaps between punchlines where the comedian has to go into too much detail in order for the joke to work – should be avoided. If you need to explain the gag too much you should either rewrite it or consider dropping it. The length of the joke's preamble must be justified by the strength of the punchline. If it is a long, involved story that ends with a feeble pun, forget it, for you will bore the audience and waste their time. If the subject is too specialist – *Krull*, tort law or the exchange-rate mechanism – bin it, because you will bore the audience. These specialist gags are fine for sci-fi conventions or corporate gigs but not for comedy clubs. The material needs to be universal not specialised, and your set needs to be well structured, with the laughs distributed evenly and regularly.

Alienating the audience

Friends are enemies you haven't alienated yet. *Anon*

Audiences are alienated by being bored or insulted or having to suffer material that is either inappropriate or poor. It is when they do not relate to you or what you are saying that you alienate them. Gross-out humour, prejudices, or outright offensiveness are comic tools that can be used effectively, but you need the experience to know how and when to use them if you want the audience to stay onside. If you alienate the audience with this kind of material then it is going to be very difficult to win them back, so either cut to the closer or wrap it up quickly. A comedy-club audience is predisposed to laughter but if you annoy them, they will decide not to laugh and that's it. Over.

What is improv?

The thing I love most is coming off the script. *Rob Newman*[7]

In live comedy, improv, or improvisation, is the ability to think in the moment and react with a comic response to a heckler, to something going wrong, or to some other distraction outside the performance script and still get a laugh out of it. Improv is not just making things up on the spot but is the ability to use things we have already said and done, or seen others say and do, to our advantage, so that we come out on top of the situation or interruption. Anyone who is considering performing live comedy should already be confident in their improvisational abilities – we usually find out that we are funny by our spontaneous responses in everyday interactions, when our friends mock us or when we have to cope with the unexpected and end up gratified by the result. This is improv: taking what is presented to us and turning it to our advantage in order to win over the audience. If we fail to deal with someone smashing a glass or tripping over drunk, we may lose favour with the audience by showing we are not up to the task.

In many recorded performances the comedian will be seen to pick on someone in the audience as if it is spontaneous. But it is in fact part of the act and based on fairly common attributes. Frankie Boyle and Richard Herring have both used bearded men in the audience to start off a sequence on paedophiles. This introduces the subject with an apparently spontaneous comment and involves the audience in the moment. It is a trick and one we should be aware of and use ourselves.

In any live comedy performance there will always be someone in the audience who stands out because of what they're wearing, what they look like or what they're doing to annoy you. The ability to identify this individual without alienating the audience or creating a violent impulse in the intended target while still getting a laugh out of it is testament to your improv skills. Effective improv involves deciding not only when to say it but also how appropriate it is to the moment. You may come on and see someone in the front row seemingly ripe to pick on, but if the comment is too strong or hurtful then it risks alienating the audience and angering the individual. This will make it harder to win back the audience and get them into your material, so improv also needs to be considerate as well as spontaneous and appropriate.

It is difficult to 'practise' improv on your own but you should have the confidence to be able to deal with the unplanned in everyday life and transfer that ability to the stage. On the comedy degree course I run, we use improv exercises where someone takes the floor and has to field any heckles or comments the other students make for a minute. This sharpens up the reflexes and makes people think on their feet. However, not every comedian is comfortable with it, so make sure you have a few stand-by comments in case of noises or interruptions.

The godfather of alternative comedy, Tony Allen, writes: 'Stand-up comedy, which is defined by its Now Agenda, can give the appearance of being wholly improvised. In reality, of course, very little is spontaneous and it is only the potential for spontaneity that exists.'[8]

The Now Agenda works for the audience as well as the performer: there is almost a subconscious collusion to maintain the atmosphere of spontaneity despite the fact that the whole performance is pre-planned. One of the attractions of live comedy to an audience is the feeling of spontaneity, that this is being created right before our eyes even though we know that it is just an act.

Some people unfamiliar with the conventions of live comedy *do* believe the comedian is simply making it up on the spot, and some comedians started out suffering from the same illusion – that somehow the material arrives fully formed when they set foot on the stage. Veteran alternative comedian Arnold Brown first performed in the early days of London's Comedy Store in 1979: 'I must have been clinically insane, because I thought that when I went on I would have an act. I had one joke in mind.'[9] Comic, writer and broadcaster Arthur Smith confessed to a similar mental block at the same venue shortly after: 'I had three one-liners and somehow thought that would fill up twenty minutes.'[10]

Even surreal comedian Ross Noble, whose act is partly improvised, has worked on the material in some shape beforehand, altering the wording or using different punch-lines. In an interview with Paramount TV, Noble spoke of levels of preparedness, saying that he often goes on stage having prepared nothing at all. According to him, part of the thrill comes from taking an idea, playing with it and seeing where it goes.

Of course, Noble has performed stand-up for many years and has a large backlog of material and experience to draw on, as well as understanding the flexibility of routines that can be adapted, punchlines that can be incorporated and a gift for genuine spontaneity. The revolutionary American comedian Lenny Bruce spoke about ad libs: 'If I do an hour show, if I'm extremely fertile, there will be about fifteen minutes of pure ad lib. But on average it's about four or five minutes. But the fact that I've created it in ad lib seems to give it a complete feeling of free form.'[11]

Comedians have differing feelings about improv. Frank Skinner actively encourages the audience to interact: 'If an audience is quiet, I'll encourage them to talk to me . . . I don't want to shut them up – I want them to give me more.'[12] Having a quantity of material, experience and spontaneous wit meant that Skinner could get off the script and create fresh new material that related to the immediate environment. Although technically the material may not be as clever or funny as the prepared stuff, the fact that the audience knows it has been newly minted gives an added quality to it: its value is its spontaneity. The audience and comedian share the moment and this is one of the best things about performing live comedy: it becomes particularly exciting when the prepared material is jettisoned through a generous interaction with the audience and there is a moment of genuine spontaneity that can never be repeated. It cannot be predicted and we can never guess the reactions of the audience and how the comedian will deal with them. It is worth again quoting Arthur Smith, who spoke about a spontaneous street performance late at night in Edinburgh: 'That's what live comedy has over telly or theatre, because at any moment the script can change, and on this occasion, I ad-libbed the whole thing anyway . . . It was more the uniqueness of the event.'[13]

Bullying the audience

At a gig, 'going among the people' is fine. Talk to the people in the front row of the audience, ask them things, for they will, in the main, enjoy it and respond. This is good improv, generating laughs from the people who are there and the situation you are in. People who sit in the front row do not usually mind: if they did, they would be at the back. Engaging with one or two audience members is a good way to put you and your audience at ease and gives the set an immediacy which seems less contrived. However, picking on someone who cannot take it will lose you sympathy and make the audience see you as a bully. There is a fine line to be drawn here and we should be careful not to cross it, as there is a big difference between gentle mockery and insults. Calling someone in the audience 'a fat b******' insults the obese as well as all the other fat b******s in the audience.

Interruptions and hecklers

Improv is a skill that takes time and experience to develop, but any comedian should be able to deal with this onstage if they can deal with it in the pub or at work. The main thing is to be confident that you can deal with it. Run through the possibilities that may interrupt you while you're onstage and create a list of responses to them. For example, someone dropping a drink or sneezing, or their mobile phone going off, someone walking across the front of the stage (your territory) or yawning in the front row. These are things you should be prepared for but not scared of. Like hecklers.

They're an odd bunch, hecklers; tell me about it. Some of the most unattractive human beings I have ever encountered have been hecklers. *Tony Allen*[14]

As well as improvisation, audience participation gives the performance its essential live quality, and we should deal with heckling in a positive manner. For most novice comedians heckling is a considerable worry. Here, various comedians discuss their experiences. For Oliver Double, the best way to deal with a heckler is by having the right mindset: 'Answering a heckler is all a matter of not showing fear, of showing that you are still in control of the situation.'[15] If you can handle a put-down in everyday life – which you should, you are funny after all – then you should be able to handle one while performing live comedy. Many comedians have stock put-downs for hecklers but some of these may be too strong for the situation. There are different kinds of heckle and each heckle is best gauged individually so that the best response can be given. For many comedians a spontaneous response is preferable to something already prepared, as it is natural to the moment.

What is heckling?

Heckling is the registration of dissent. Even good-natured heckling detracts from the performer-audience relationship because the heckler is imposing on the performance. A lot of heckling is poor-quality: especially drunk audience members shouting. But some heckling is genuinely witty. A good comedian can build this into the act and it is important to do so. As Oliver Double says, 'To ignore it is to seriously undermine the audience's faith . . . the illusion of spontaneity is broken'.[16] The response to the heckler must be appropriate to the degree of hostility in the heckle, but the response should also be appropriate for the comedian's persona. As Harry Hill pointed out, 'You can't just say "f*** off", you know'.[17] The Hill persona/character does not have this in his vocabulary, so he must find a more suitable reaction which does not break 'character'.

Learn to love your heckler

I still get plenty of heckling. It's good in that it does something to the atmosphere of a show, and on occasions it can lift it up on to another level and make the audience feel more involved. *Jo Brand* [18]

For many people who want to try performing live comedy for the first time, the heckler becomes a concern that gets out of all proportion so that they are put off entirely by the threat of it. It is an important part of live comedy, so much so that William Cook's book *Ha Bloody Ha: Comedians Talking* devotes an entire section to it. Heckling is a vital test for the comedian and it gives the audience a chance to get involved. Most comedians do the same set night after night so it makes them more 'live'. A lot of heckling is pointless and destructive but it can really make a gig if done right. It is here that any improvisation skills come in handy.

There is something of a myth about heckling. It's often suggested that every comedy club has a throng of hecklers making clever, witty remarks . . . I might have heard three or four funny heckles. Mostly it's just drunks shouting 'f*** off' or just making incomprehensible noises and then falling over. *Frank Skinner* [19]

British comedian Jo Brand says her favourite heckle was someone shouting out, about her short leggings: 'Why don't you put some jam on your shoes and invite your trousers to tea?'[20] Comedian and writer Hannah George has noted a gender difference in heckling. 'I never really get heckled that much, but a lot of the time it'll be blokes that do it. Mostly blokes'll be showing off to their mates, so when you can come back with a biting remark it's brilliant. I quite like being heckled by blokes for being a woman, as it gives you an opportunity to show them exactly what you're made of.' Magician Ian Saville sees a positive aspect to heckling: 'Mostly

I find they are good-natured. I try not to get into confrontations, and when they come up with a good line I give them the credit (at that performance – I might use it again myself later).' Disabled comedian Mat Fraser views hecklers as an integral part of a performance:

I love them, they are fuel to my fire. When it's really good they can run like a vein through your set . . . except a really weird recent one where all the very drunk and badly timed guy did was compliment me, in a condescending way, so just as I hit a punchline he would shout over me, 'Very good, you're doing well! Keep going.' It disarmed me, to be honest, hahaha, bad choice of phrase perhaps but I should have gone in harder on him I guess.

For ventriloquist Paul Zerdin, 'Hecklers are brilliant, they can really liven a night up.' For Brighton-based drag act Davina Sparkle, heckling is a fact of life:

Sometimes leery drunk people are not worth putting down as they make a prat of themselves anyway, but having some really good one-liner put-downs in your repertoire will always help. If the person continues, or someone thinks they're smart, being prepared is the key, but don't make the mistake of making the show about the heckler. Continue to ignore them and they usually shut up!

Negative heckling

Jo Brand has a lot of tales of nasty and abusive heckling that many would be ill-equipped to deal with, but these tend to be rarer. Not everyone sees the comic value of hecklers and different countries have different attitudes. For UK-based German stand-up Henning Wehn, 'Hecklers usually shout the same things. I get loads of heckles like 5.1 football scores but I prepare answers for things I have already been heckled with.'

David Kiliminick, who runs the Off The Wall comedy club in Jerusalem, has a far less forgiving attitude towards them:

Hecklers just keep the express train from moving, constantly stop and go. They stop the audience from enjoying, and they don't usually enjoy it either – unless they are sick people, who get a rise out of ruining everybody's evening. A heckler is somebody with low self-esteem, who has something to prove. A heckler is usually the one person who has no idea what the show is about. People who are insecure and can't accept that other people are funny should not come to shows. I don't think they should leave their homes.

Not everyone gets heckled or if they do it is relatively rare. Shazia Mirza says, 'I have been heckled but not much and not badly. They've often just been drunk or stupid.' Props comic George Egg also says, 'I don't get heckled very much. I don't like it when I do but I'll deal with it quickly, politely and (hopefully) efficiently. My show doesn't invite heckling like some performers' shows do, and I think it's because I'm clearly performing a written/devised "show" rather than creating the illusion of chatting and making it up as I go along, as is the case with a lot of regular stand-up.' George has also noticed that 'I get heckled less and less as I've got older, and I wonder if that's down to me improving as an act or if it's a physical thing and the fact that I'm older than the audience.' Stephen Rosenfeld of the American Comedy Institute in New York says, 'There are fewer hecklers [in the US] than in the UK. Most shows don't have hecklers.'

The heckling tradition in the UK is a long and robust one that goes back to Elizabethan times, and probably earlier. The early performances of Shakespeare were subject to rowdy audiences just as much as the lesser playwrights' work was. This continued into the music hall and is all part of British 'rough theatre' (to plagiarise Peter Brook's *The Empty Space*).

The American tradition of live comedy performance is a different one, although vaudeville was probably just as rough as UK music hall. As modern live comedy in the States was developing in the Catskills holiday resorts and the metropolitan theatres and clubs, heckling did not become an integral part of the performance but more of an unwanted interruption. That is very different from the inevitable hazard that it is in Britain. So although there will be heckling at some point in your career, remember that it does not happen at every gig. If it does, you will need to have the improv skills or prepared put-downs to cope with it easily, so that anything that hecklers throw at you can be incorporated into the act.

Prepared put-downs

All hecklers, like all gigs and audiences, are different. Be prepared with a selection of put-downs ranging from mild to devastating. Most hecklers want to be involved in the show and they are audience members so should be acknowledged – just watch that they don't go over the line. When dealing with an annoying and negative heckler, remember that you will usually have the audience onside, because the heckler is disrupting the audience's night out. Just be prepared and use put-downs appropriate to the degree of heckling. Also, stop obsessing: it rarely happens and if it does you will be able to deal with it like any other day-to-day interruption. They rarely have more than one good heckle and you have had plenty of time to think of better ones. London-based comedian Donna McPhail cites the most useful advice about heckling given to her by the godfather of alternative comedy, Tony Allen: 'Never assume a heckler is cleverer than you. They might manage to come out with one fairly witty line – but if you can come out with one back, you've won. And if you don't try, you've lost anyway – so you've got nothing to lose.'[21]

Tolerance

Not all heckling is by drunks imposing their fragile egos on things. Audience members will heckle if the subject matter of the jokes goes beyond what they see as acceptable. Most audiences are tolerant of the majority of things, as many comedy-audience members are familiar with the conventions. It is the comedian's job to read the audience and monitor the previous acts and the MC to see what the audience responds to and what their limits of tolerance are. The limit of tolerance is how far an audience is prepared to go along with a particular idea, and it brings into question the issues of shock value, morality and offensiveness. Risqué jokes about child abuse are not going to go down well at the Children's Society Christmas party. There has often been the need to remind the audience, 'It's just a joke!' But is it? We need to ensure that our material is read by the audience in the way we intended it to be.

Face value?

In the 1960s and 1970s there was a British TV programme called *Till Death Us Do Part*, which featured a racist bigot called Alf Garnett. The character was meant to be a satire on such attitudes, but many people took him at face value because he articulated some of their more offensive beliefs. Contemporary comedians such as the American Sarah Silverman and the British Jimmy Carr and Al Murray perform what could be called 'offensive comedy', comedy that deals with taboo subjects. Although they say they are doing this ironically – that is, they do not really mean it but are satirising the points (which can often sound unconvincing in some cases) – many of the audience members take the joke at face value. They laugh at the joke about different races or the homeless because it confirms their prejudices, despite the fact that it was meant as an 'ironic' statement. The problem with 'ironic offensiveness' is that some people will always take it at face value; the intended meaning of any ironic statement is always the exact opposite of its literal meaning.

How do we get people to understand the joke in the way it was intended? We have to consider this when thinking about doing ironic or offensive material: is the actual intention clear or are we just passing off an offensive gag for easy laughs and getting away with it because it is cloaked in irony? It is perhaps too easy to do risqué material and then claim it was 'ironic' when it backfires. Scottish comedian Frankie Boyle is well known for his 'offensive' material but he is also a very experienced performer who can do other kinds of material. In addition, we need to make sure that this is not the whole of the show but only one aspect of a more varied set. Being offensive gets wearing after a while – for performers and audiences alike.

The meaning of any joke is ultimately in the audience members' interpretation. This is an ethical situation: how do we perform such material and avoid misinterpretation that confirms prejudice? We will consider this next.

Offensiveness

Offensiveness is a powerful comic tool when used onstage. Outraging people's sensibilities is risky and needs to be done carefully. We need the audience to like us and go along with (much) of what we say. Some audience members may become uncomfortable with certain material and the comedian may lose them. And, as we have seen, it is difficult winning back the favour of an audience if they consider you to hold beliefs that they find offensive. We need to pick our targets carefully. On the UK stand-up circuit at the moment it is, apparently, okay to do jokes about disabled people, gay people or foreigners – so long as it is done ironically. However, the last taboo is racism and if a comedian does 'ironically racist' material, then they can find themselves in difficulties. Racism is unpleasant for many audience members and they do not want to be seen as complicit in supporting such material.

Sarah Silverman is a good case study here. She presents a semi-innocent stage persona while doling out jokes that can be seen as offensive. She emphasises her Jewishness in order to be seen as a minority rather than a member of the majority having a go at other minorities. (Comedy is at its best when it attacks those who are our 'superiors' but having a go at those who are in a weaker position than we are takes us back to bullying.) Silverman's delivery depends on the audience understanding that she does not really mean it, that this is irony. However, not everyone sees it like that. As she admits in her autobiography, an old-school comedian came up to her and told her she had 'the best n***** jokes'. Unbeknown to Silverman, her material had merely been confirming his prejudices and he took her words at face value.

This has happened to many comedians who do offensive material: audience members have come up to them and told even more extreme jokes because they have not realised the irony and think that the comedian means it and shares their prejudices. When we do this kind of material, we have to be careful that people understand it in the way it is intended. All audiences are different and all audience members more so!

Recap

We need to establish a relationship with the audience and make sure they understand who we are and what we are doing. Audience members should be our friends. Get them onside fast by being funny first. Remember:
• There are good audiences and bad.
• Sometimes it is not our fault our set does not go over well,

but when it is our fault, we need to admit it and act fast.
- Read the room: make sure the material is appropriate.
- Do not embarrass the audience by being amateurish – get off!
- Do not bore the audience with your specialisms – get off!
- Do not alienate them by grossing them out – get off!
- Do not bully or insult the audience. If they do not like you – get off!
- Hecklers are not all bad so learn to love them.
- Hecklers can make the night so learn to love them.
- Hecklers usually only have one line but if the heckler is funnier than you – get off!
- Prepare put-downs that vary in degrees of savagery.
- If you are doing a character or being 'ironic', make sure the audience is clear about this and *do not* let them take it at face value. If they do – get off and get a taxi quick!

9. The Comedy Industry

Comedy is a multi-billion dollar global industry that shows no sign of shrinking. It has never before been so pluralistic, with festivals, specialist TV channels and an exciting global market for live work featuring comedians of all ages and all styles. The world of comedy has venues to suit all performers at every stage of the game, from open-mic nights to well established 'big' names in large theatres, for everyone from old-school gag merchants to new and controversial comedians. It has never been so exciting. What's more, the audience is now more varied than it has ever been, with specific venues catering for particular crowds who all have different comedy tastes.

Live comedy is here to stay and it is important to understand how the industry works and how it is organised so we can become more professional and enhance the chances of our success. Writing and performing comedy are the relatively easy bits. There are many other people behind the scenes who make things happen, who determine where comedians perform and what kinds of things are said onstage. It is important to have a working knowledge of this, and it will be covered in this chapter.

Marketing yourself

First, though, you need to decide how you are going to market yourself. You are selling yourself, after all. So who are you aiming your act at? What style are you going to present to your audience (bearing in mind that styles do evolve over time)? And what kind of material do you intend to do? A simplification you can use is 'are we cult or are we clean?'

Cult or mainstream?

Very broadly speaking, there are two main strands of comedy, the mainstream and the cult. It is important to understand who we want to communicate with in live comedy, who our potential audience is, and what they will relate to. In the 1980s and 1990s in the US and the UK, it was quite easy to differentiate between mainstream and alternative comedy, but now those who come from the alternative legacy are the mainstream, and the trad comedians are now much more marginalised. Generally speaking, mainstream comedians are those on panel shows or stand-up specials or who dominate the more popular sitcoms.

There are instances, however, where the more traditional comedians work with 'alternative' comedians. For example, on BBC Radio 4's *Just A Minute,* comedy improvisers Paul Merton and Ross Noble appear alongside old-timer television presenter Nicholas Parsons. *Just A Minute* likewise presents comedy godfather Barry Cryer and assorted former members of *The Goodies* as well as Jack Dee, who began at The Comedy Store, and Stephen Fry, who started out at Cambridge Footlights and then appeared on British TV series *Saturday Live*, hosted by Ben Elton in the 1980s. These are good examples of different but compatible comedy styles working together.

Cult comedy aims at a smaller, less mainstream audience,

who share the same frame of reference and experiences as the writers and performers. Cult comedy can deal with obscure or black humour such as Harold & Maude, or it can be quite close to the mainstream like the Coen brothers' better comedies: it can be a box-office flop and home-viewing success, or be just as lucrative as mainstream comedy on its initial release. There are many cult films, such as *Wayne's World*, *Withnail & I* and *The Big Lebowski* which may be familiar to many comedy fans, and these have their own cult followings. They were never likely to garner the success of a more mainstream Hugh Grant movie, but there again they never intended to. Cult comedy is defined by its subject matter and style (slang, cultural references). Both *Trainspotting* and *Withnail & I* deal with substance abuse by people on the margins of society. *The Big Lebowski* is a neo-*film noir* set in a bowling alley, with a pot-smoking idler as the lead. Hardly mainstream. Some cult sitcoms like *Curb Your Enthusiasm* or *My Name Is Earl* are likewise about marginalised characters who are not generally white, middle-class suburbanites.

In live comedy there is also a strong thread of the cult that, although successful, has not crossed over into the mainstream, such as musical stand-up Demetri Martin, surrealist duo The Mighty Boosh, and others who are unlikely to be guests on mainstream panel shows. The British anti-comedian Ed Aczel is an example. Perfectly content to do his own thing, Aczel says, 'I never wanted to be particularly conventional.' Ed Aczel prefers his one-man shows at Edinburgh because 'there's so much you can try out. I feel far more at home. I feel very constricted in a club environment, claustrophobic in some way. It's your space and your time. People come to see you.' Identifying who the potential audience is and performing material that is not compromised and aimed at them is part of maintaining cult status. It is also about smaller audience numbers.

The British stand-up Daniel Kitson has earned a devoted audience the hard way – by sticking to what he thinks is the right thing for him. He has spoken about his dislike of working on the sitcom *Peter Kay's Phoenix Nights* and other television work because of the restrictions of the medium and the lack of control the comedian has over the final product. At his own shows he can determine how things run, and he performs in his own inimitable way, doing a mix of stand-up and story-telling. He has worked hard to build up his own audience, who are prepared to follow him away from the traditional gag-gag-gag style of much comedy.

You choose

You must decide: are you going for cult status or are you aiming for the more lucrative mainstream? However, starting off as an oddball cult character onstage does not mean that it is unpalatable for the mainstream. Look at the success of Harry Hill. He started off as a very cult act but endeavoured and is now hosting peak-time TV shows. Ask yourself these questions:

- Am I a cult?
- What is the style and subject matter of the act? Do I talk about specialised subjects? Is it surreal? Absurd?
- What is my stage persona? Is it accessible?
- Would my mum get it or is it out there like Emo Philips or Demetri Martin?

Keeping it clean (or not)

The major changes that alternative comedy brought about in America and the UK were in subject matter and language. Alternative comedy, and much stand-up comedy today, is aimed at an audience ranging from eighteen to forty, and it deals with the things that concern them: relationships, such as sex, drugs, drinking, politics, work. It is not uncommon for comedians to use what the vanguard of televisual morality calls 'strong language'. People swear – it is a fact of life. Also, swearing can accentuate a punchline and make the joke more effective.

However, there are comedians who never use strong language or deal with dodgy subjects. Jerry Seinfeld has an accessible Everyman attitude and talks about universal things that anyone anywhere can understand. He discusses things that students, his parents and both men and women can relate to, and it is this that has made him the success he is today. Harry Hill and Tim Vine are other examples. Hill never swears onstage or discusses anything graphic or controversial. His accessible, if odd, stage character has made the successful transition from the stand-up stage to hosting his own *TV Burp* show and *You've Been Framed*. He is recognised as a mainstream, 'family-friendly' presenter and has also gained some success in America which a lot of British comedians find elusive. Brit pun-artist Tim Vine is likewise family-friendly, and his endless barrage of gags and one-liners never strays into controversial territory. His easy-going stage presence and absurd view of the world have made him a household name.

The choice of subject matter, stage persona and language will determine who your eventual audience is going to be. Your audience will choose you. Obviously, at a typical comedy club several comedians are on the bill and the core audience is there to see live comedy rather than a particular act. But whoever else is on the bill, we still need a clear sense of identity so we can communicate with our audiences. Maintaining an identity offstage is essential. Therefore, we have to decide what we are going to talk about, who our potential audience is and what level of venues we can expect to perform at. Although the comedy market is extremely varied, comedians are not always able to transplant their acts into different comedy venues. The main thing, though, is to be true to yourself.

Branding

There must be something there first that you can sell. *Henning Wehn*

We need to present an image, a style of presentation, to sell as a package if we are serious about a career in the comedy industry, so one of the most important questions any comedian needs to ask is 'who am I and what do I do?' The audience, too, needs a clear idea of who you are and what to expect. They have to be able to discern one act from another, so performers need to emphasise what makes them different from the person onstage before and after them. Once we have decided what our act and persona are going to be, then we need to think in terms of branding. By understanding certain elements of our stage persona, we can take what is special about us and what sets us apart and then amplify them for publicity reasons.

We need to build an audience who recognise our names and know what we do. This can obviously take some time but it helps an audience identify a particular performer if there is something unique about them. The advantage of vent acts, musical acts or double acts is their relative rarity – they stand out on any bill of solo performers. If we have nothing in our act to distinguish it, such as musical instruments or props, then physical attributes can be useful. An accent can be an advantage too, especially if the gig is not local to the comedian, as much live comedy is a verbal medium. The way we talk and certain terms we use will be different. Rich Hall delivers his material slowly in a dry, gravelly voice that is very recognisable. A Scottish performer in London has an 'away' advantage because of the way they speak. A Liverpool accent is also recognisable and can be used to advantage: old Scouse comedian Stan Boardman got great comic mileage out of repeatedly saying 'Fokkers' and 'Geeermans' in an exaggerated Liverpool accent. Peter Kay did likewise with his catchphrase 'giz a phone!' which is very Northern English.

If interesting comedy is based on being told what we do not know already or having recognisable things discussed in a new way, then regional differences can be useful. Explaining the idiosyncrasies of our home towns is valuable material but they must be things the audience recognise or understand and cannot be too specialised. It is also important not to self-parody and get cheap laughs by confirming stereotypes of drunken Australians, aggressive New Yorkers or pie-and-mash cockney geezers. There has to be a universal subject despite local differences (families, relationships), hence the success of Peter Kay.

Who do you think you are?

So, who are you? What are you selling? What is your angle? Where are you from? And how do you use it in a recognisable, accessible package?

Photographs and publicity

Although live comedy tends to be a more verbal form of entertainment, there is still a visual element to the performance and we need to acknowledge this when we are 'branding' ourselves. It is all part of the package. When we perform, people look at us as well as listening and we can use this in our favour. Comedians vary from the almost world-weary and cynical like Louis CK, the transvestite Eddie Izzard or the big-collared Harry Hill. Props, costumes and musical instruments add a visual and physical dimension to the performance – if you can play something like the banjo or you can juggle, put it in the act and the publicity, even if you only do one gag with it. Make sure when people see your Facebook page or gig flyer that it is prominent, so folks in the future say, 'Oh, it's the guy with the accordion/ventriloquist dummy/firework-up-the-arse finale [Londoner Chris Lynam]. They were good.'

You will need some photographs to put on websites, posters and other publicity material. If you are tall, emphasise this. The British comedian and writer Miranda Hart has built her public image into a large and clumsy persona. She communicates the difficulty of being a tall woman through her material. If you are small, you can do likewise. Remember, if you have a noticeable physical characteristic, audiences will expect you to comment on this – so do it before they do. The musical Aussie comedian Tim Minchin's publicity emphasises his wild hair and eye make-up, making him instantly recognisable. The Brit-based German comedian Henning Wehn wears a distinct stage outfit with a stopwatch round his neck which is part of the opening of his act, and he wears it in his publicity pictures too.

The most overused image is the mic and spotlight, so use this wisely. On the cover of one of Chris Rock's DVDs, *Bigger and Blacker*, Rock is shown gripping a 1950s mic and staring aggressively into the camera, backdropped by a bare brick wall. This image tells you exactly what you are going to get: a forthright black guy, doing confrontational, no-frills stand-up. This approach would not work with someone like Daniel Kitson or Demetri Martin. The image has to be appropriate and to communicate the style of comedy. One of Stewart Lee's publicity shots shows him looking quizzically through a hangman's noose. It is a mix of black humour and absurdity. Bill Bailey's DVD covers and tour publicity show him as a faintly perplexed, long-haired, genial character, which does not contradict his live performances. Lee Evans's publicity emphasises his physical elasticity. Be careful when choosing PR images. Look at what others have done by all means, but avoid copying them, and try to use photographs that amplify your physical characteristics.

Photo fit

Ask yourself these questions when choosing your publicity photos:

- What are my most noticeable physical attributes: Hair? Bald? Tall/short? Thin/fat?
- Is there anything I can emphasise to make me more distinctive?
- Can I use a prop in order to distinguish me from others in my publicity and on websites?
- Does the image presented in the photos reflect the kind of comedy I do? For example, aggressive (like Chris Rock)? Bizarre (like Harry Hill)?

If you get any reviews, clip them and add them to your publicity. If you can get other comedians that you have performed with to say something nice about you, then do so. The more comments from comedians and venues the better. Having a tagline is also helpful regarding publicity, flyers, posters and websites: 'Stewart Lee bills himself as Officially the 41st-best Stand-Up Ever' is a good handle. Anonymity is not a good marketing tool and we need to emphasise distinctiveness as well as style in all of our choices. The more coherent and consistent the name, tagline and image, the better the brand.

If you are going to use a particular photo, obviously make sure it's a good one and that you have e-copies in different formats, for people to copy-and-paste into other websites and publicity. You could always use Photoshop or a similar program to enhance it and turn it from a simple head shot into a viable and instantly recognisable image.

Agents

At this stage of your career, agents are probably not a major concern but it is useful to know what they actually do. Matt Willetts, who runs Comicus Ltd – a booking agency special-ising in securing gigs for comedians at corporate events, private gigs and on cruise ships as well as organising comedy nights at other venues – offers some sound advice on what agents look for when booking various gigs. According to Matt, as a comedian you should 'be completely true to yourself. Do not try and be someone else, like your comedy hero, but entertain an audience with the material you find funny. But be patient, building a strong act takes time.' For Matt there is no such thing as a good comedian because each gig is different. Booking them depends on 'whether the comedian is ready and suits the work you have for them. No one comedian is right for every single job or gig.' As far as booking corporate gigs is concerned, he says that 'comedians need to be clean (no swearing or heavy adult content) and need to have a certain style that matches the event, a professional persona. At the same time they still need to have an edge.' With regard to booking cruise ships he says, 'The comic must be absolutely clean, no swearing or heavy adult content again. They should be able to entertain and engage a family audience with straightforward, mainstream, non-controversial material.' So having an ability to adapt the material to different audiences while not overly compromising is key here.

Maintaining an Internet presence

Apart from television, the Internet is where many people access comedians, and we need to maintain a web profile to capitalise on this.

Facebook

Nowadays there are plenty of social networks and free packages to use as contact points and social-networking sites like Facebook are easily accessible. Rather than having cumbersome and corny business cards we can now say to interested folk at gigs 'I'm on Facebook' and sign them up as friends whom we can keep informed of our current activities. We can build a community of interested people and also share information on gigs, experience and other comedians (though no gossip – it may come back and bite you). Facebook helpfully suggests other 'friends' and comedians often pop up. Keep in touch with people all round the world: you never know when the information will come in useful.

YouTube

YouTube is an excellent source for comedy geeks to find obscure clips and rave about them, and it is also a site on which many people surf. The tags that people put on their own clips will mean they pop up when someone is looking for something else, which is when we find comedy gems from past and present. Setting up a YouTube account and putting clips of you performing is easy. You can film them on a cheap digital camera (in fact, some venues do this anyway, so get a copy). You can edit a five-minute performance down to a couple of gags that are the highlights of your set and that got a good reception. Even if you have only recorded the sound (remember that digital dictaphone?) then you can still make a clip using footage or stills of things that complement what you are talking about. Use your imagination. It is also useful to read what people have said about your clips. Hopefully these will be supportive or useful and if they aren't, well, what do the public know anyway? Use the clips to emphasise your style.

Blogs

In 2002, bored at work and turning thirty, American Julie Powell decided she wanted to write a blog but didn't know what to write about. She quickly realised that she needed a long-term project to use as her subject matter and decided to cook all 524 recipes from Julia Childs's classic cookbook, *Mastering the Art of French Cooking*, 'for the servantless American cook'. Powell decided to cook all the recipes one by one and write up the experience every day in her blog, giving herself a one-year deadline. This gave the blog a purpose as well as a structure. Each daily entry for the blog was a single episode that gradually built up to an overall narrative. Each episode involved a task with a high risk of failure but it also included her feelings about how she was faring, both in the kitchen and personally. The reader not only learned about her culinary endeavours but also developed a relationship with her as she faced struggles similar to the reader's own in her everyday life. Eventually, Julie cooked her way through all the recipes and along the way built up a dedicated readership. Her readers could relate to the subject of food as well as the difficulties that preparing a successful meal entails: it was not just about food but about human endeavour. The blog was a success and became a book, and the book was a success and became a comedy film, starring Meryl Streep.

But what can we learn from Julie? Although we cannot all hope to replicate her success, we can pick up a few tips to help us maintain our public profiles as well as improve our writing skills. If we keep a blog for a year, say, that documents our development as a comedian and writer, then there is an overall purpose. Potential readers are curious and naturally want to see whether our career succeeds or fails, or even just whether we can actually keep the blog going for a year. If we document every writing session and performance, then each entry becomes inherently interesting, like a gag, that fits into an overall narrative, like a set. It has a purpose, a process and a climax. For us, the blog involves the discipline of writing every day. There is a commitment made to ourselves as well as our readers which we have to stick to.

Writing every day will improve our skills as a writer, as we learn to write economically, succinctly and accurately. We set ourselves short-term, achievable goals, like a gig or even just a joke every day, as well as a long-term goal which gives the blog narrative sense. Being in the habit of writing regularly, even if what you write is just an exercise, can only help. The great American writer John Steinbeck suffered from regular writer's block. To combat this he used to write 'poetry for throwing away': it was meant as arm exercise rather than for public consumption. The blog is a good exercise in this respect.

A blog is easy to set up, even for the biggest techno-klutz, and requires very few design skills (Wordpress does a free version that is suitable for this purpose). It doesn't have to be flashy, just interesting to read. It needs fresh material to justify people coming back, so charting your progress, gig by gig, writing session by session, and asking for input on what readers think of new material are all extremely useful.

A bonus is that it will give you an idea of how far you have come, from the trembling neophyte before the first gig to a hardened, widely experienced comedian a year later. And if you carry on writing the blog, it will continue to document your progress as you build up your career performing live comedy.

Adding links to clips of your act on YouTube, and to any

other website you have been on or you just like, is also useful. This again helps build up a community of friends whose feedback can become invaluable. Every time you send an email, put the blog address at the bottom of the message to encourage traffic. Be active on the web. At gigs, talk to other comedians and keep in touch via these free mediums. Share information, such as warnings about dangerous audiences or smelly venues (or indeed smelly audiences and dangerous venues).

The blog is a good way of getting information to potential audiences on where you are going to perform in the future. Blogs, like Facebook, YouTube pages and Twitter, are also invaluable for the comedian because people browse them and can come across your name easily. Just remember the gimmick, a good profile name and photo that people will recognise. Ed Aczel's befuddled face makes him look like someone who would wear their trousers inside out and not notice. His unusual name and style of delivery are examples of good marketing. As is Jimmy Carr's publicity material, which is slick and neat. Like him.

Gaining fans through a blog

Remember these tips if you start blogging:
- Be truthful about your failures as well as your successes. Do not try to talk up something that did not really work.
- Be regular. If you are erratic, you will lose your readers. When people access your blog and it hasn't changed since the last time they looked, then they will soon delete it from their favourites as a dead site.
- Ask for feedback and if you get a response, answer it quickly. Enter into dialogue with people, as their opinions are important: they are your readers and are probably comedy geeks like us!

Building up gigs

We need to use publicity as a way to maintain an offstage profile but it also helps in securing gigs at places we have yet to play. If you email asking for a gig, be sure to include your website, blog or Facebook page in the message as well as in any other relevant publicity material. We need to build up a regular circuit of gigs, both those where we have performed before as well as new places. If you have followed all the excellent advice in this book, you will no doubt have stormed your first gig – so, as for any other gig that has gone well (or even just ok), ask the organiser if you can come back again to do another spot. Give it a few weeks so you can go back with some new material. Do not arrange it for the following week and then turn up and do exactly what you did last time. You need time to readjust your set and include new gags.

This is a pattern you need to develop as you go along: every time you do a gig well and the audience related to you, ask for another gig. They will usually say yes, as they will always have future gigs to fill. Assess each individual gig and make life easier for yourself: if you died on your arse first time there, then don't see it as a 'challenge' to go back to eventually win the audience over. It simply isn't your gig, so find another spot. However, with crap gigs as well as good ones, record your thoughts on your blog or in your notebook. That way you can reassess the situation at a later date and see if you can do the gig better when you have a bit more experience.

Keeping a diary of upcoming dates makes you feel more confident and professional. Soon you will have gigs booked in for the next few months, and as you do these, you'll find others, building up your own set of gigs where you can do well. Keep your diary scrupulously so you know where you are going to be in the future months and you avoid getting double-booked. Be organised and think ahead, not just by the week or by the month but looking at the next six months.

If you want information about the comedy industry, the best source is other comedians. Don't be shy at gigs – speak to people. Find out where they are from, what is going on where they live and what the open-mic spots are like. It is better to get the information about gigs from comedians you have just watched than going in there blind. You will no doubt keep meeting comedians who are at the same level as you and this networking and information-sharing are essential. Also, just because someone is topping the bill – and getting paid – does not mean they are completely unapproachable. Speak to them and find out how they have got to that position. Remember, they started out doing wee open mics like you.

Open-mic spots

These are weird. Some you can storm and others make you wonder 'what am I doing this for?' Some open-mic nights are for anyone – comedians, poets or musicians – and you need to choose your venue carefully so you know the audience will be up for some comedy. If it is specifically for comedy, great. If it is for spoken word and poetry, you may do well. If it is for musicians, forget it unless you are going to MC it, when a bit of comedy always goes down well. Book a spot, and then, as already mentioned, attend the week before if possible, to see if you and your material are suitable. Open-mic spots tend to be in small venues midweek, when trade is slow and performers are a ready source of revenue for landlords. Just be careful. Check out the audience and performers in advance and you can avoid embarrassment.

If you do well at an open-mic spot, you will be invited back and maybe even offered a small amount of cash. By returning and doing well again, it could be transformed into a regular spot. Having an empty diary is depressing, so you need to take whatever work is offered to you, despite the fact that you are losing out. To expect immediate riches is delusional. Comedians rarely go into this game for money and you need to understand that while you are building your career you have to pay out to get about. Consider this an investment for the future. Self-belief is all. You know that you are funny and have something, and you need to convince people that what you are doing is worth it.

One thing to look out for is the pay-to-play policy that some unscrupulous venues are doing. This means you have to pay to get up there and perform, which ensures the organiser makes something out of the night. They may also insist that you have to bring along a certain number of people before you can perform. Do not agree to this – find somewhere else. The gig organisers Laughing Horse have this advice: 'If the phrases "pay-to-play" or "flyer-to-gig" or "bringer-show" have ever crossed your mind as a way to run a gig, please just f*** off and go and ruin another industry, thank you.'

Time Out: London

London is the centre of the UK comedy industry whether we like it or not. There are many clubs, competitions and open-mic spots and it is where producers and booking agents hang out. For comedians, *Time Out* magazine is an essential read. A weekly listings magazine, it includes the contact details and addresses of all the comedy nights and venues within the London area. For new comedians and established ones it is an essential purchase, as it is easy to book a few open spots over a couple of nights and forget about the expense. If you live in or near London, what are you waiting for? Buy the latest issue now and get calling. If you know someone in London and can stay there, great. If you know any of the other comedians on the bill, they might put you up. You only need the price of a travel card for the Tube and a few beers and you can do this on the cheap.

Ring around the venues in *Time Out* and use social-networking websites to find out what the audiences are like and what other comedians think. Start small and build it from there. In the meantime, continue doing gigs in your local area and moving around establishing yourself. Do not do The Comedy Store until you are ready. This is comedy Mecca and can be approached later when you are much more confident and experienced.

Competitions

Laughing Horse have been organising comedy events in the UK since 1998, promoting comedy and comedians as well as organising venues. They have plenty of advice for comedians who are just starting out. As far as competitions are concerned, they say:

With so many newer acts starting out in comedy these days, competitions help those that are talented get ahead of the game and raise their heads above the parapet. The larger competitions allow comedy industry people to see good new performers that may get lost in the crowd, and the bigger competitions are respected enough to help the winners get more bookings, and exposure with promoters that may otherwise not see them.

Laughing Horse know full well that the circuit needs new acts all the time and that comedians move up through the hierarchy of gigs, so there is always space for us. However, they also acknowledge that being a successful comedian involves a lot of hard work:

Comedy is incredibly popular now and people want new talent, and it is true that talent always shines through, but with so many newer acts there has to be a huge amount of desire, determination and sheer bloody-mindedness sometimes to progress through the newer act end of the comedy circuit these days – which is getting more and more akin to the wild west with poorly run nights and pay-to-play scams becoming *de rigueur* especially in London. Do well in a competition and this can help you progress with your career that much quicker.

London-based comedian Ivor Dembina, however, warns of the dangers of ending up a 'competition comic' where you tailor your material for specific judges rather than speaking in your own, authentic voices. You need to assess each gig and how helpful it is going to be as you progress through your comedy career. Winning a competition is a massive morale boost and validates your belief in yourself as a comedian, but things like the Edinburgh Fringe can be a little more daunting.

The Edinburgh Fringe

Alexei Sayle and Tony Allen were the first 'alternative comedians' to perform at the Edinburgh Festival Fringe and since then it has become one of the world's greatest events for comedy. According to Mark Fisher, author of *The Edinburgh Fringe Survival Guide*, 'For dedicated comedians . . . the Fringe is a central part of the professional calendar . . . For many comedians, the Fringe is a catalyst to up their game or to try something new'.[1] Everyone has different experiences of the Fringe but all agree it can be *the* place for an act to make a name for themselves. Julian Hall, comedy critic for the *Independent* newspaper, explained what makes a successful Edinburgh show:

It's impossible to totally nail this but a show that has some structure without looking too built, a show that has heart without being mawkish, and a show that is truthful without being psychotherapy will do well. Oh, and jokes of course, ones that you'll quote back to people for years to come. Yes, it's a big ask and that's why people still love to come and 'crack' Edinburgh.

Comedian Mat Fraser sees it as an 'expensive fun alcohol-fuelled orgiastic drug-addled booze-soaked party time, with some gigs as well. These days I just do spots in other people's shows as it's far too hard to mount your own and a thankless task of failure all too often. I would only do it now if I was produced well by someone else.'

The excessive side of the Fringe is something that Zoe Lyons agrees about. In her experience it means 'late nights, rivers of booze, terrible shows, wonderful shows, camaraderie, competitiveness, chips and rain'. Shazia Mirza finds Edinburgh 'hard. In every way. I go there to develop my craft, watch comedy, do my new show, and watch the comedians I admire. That's why I go. No one enjoys every single minute of the entire month.' Ed Aczel has found a natural home for his act, but he also sees the yearly visit as an impetus to keep writing:

If I didn't have a deadline for Edinburgh I wouldn't be writing, I'd have my head in the clouds. I've done four shows. You come up with a theme, usually in March. You have it on the back of a fag packet. All the Edinburgh brochures get done in March so all the stuff on the back of the fag packet goes into them. Then you have to write around it. You get committed to stuff you didn't want to get committed to, that was so badly thought through at the time, and suddenly you've got to make it fly.

Comedian and writer Hannah George has the following to say about the Fringe:

'Edinburgh is a massive comedian's office party. It's an amazing place to be in August: there are so many emotions flying around – vanity, ego, hatred, love, jealousy, admiration, hatred, respect, joy, hatred and a few venereal diseases. From a female perspective I've always had a lovely time in Edinburgh. My last show, 'It's Got Jokes In', was an all-female stand-up show and we honestly debated for several months whether we should risk taking it up there, as we were worried people wouldn't want to come to see three women. Luckily for us, the gamble paid off as we were pretty full every single day.

Laughing Horse run the Free Festival at Edinburgh (www. freefestival.co.uk) presenting shows across all Fringe genres – music and theatre as well as comedy. They manage venues, performance spaces and volunteers across sixteen venues and have managed 6,000 performances of shows. They also produce the daily Pick of the Fringe shows and organise comedy courses. They warn, only half-jokingly, of the usual hazards of 'a considerable amount of eating unhealthily and drinking too much!' For someone going to Edinburgh to perform for the first time, they emphasise the need for hard work and to expect 'long hours, bad reviews, awful weather, exhaustion, chaos, battling egos, huge expenses, dodgy accommodation, no sleep, enough alcohol to pickle your liver and a diet consisting solely of battered offal eaten at 3 a.m. in the morning outside takeaways'. They also say it can be the best experience of your life as well as being artistically rewarding. A typical Fringe experience 'gives every day the highs and lows of celebrating New Year's Eve, and gets repeated every day for twenty-five days. And then for completely illogical reasons you will want to return and do it all again, every year.'

So the main things to be deduced from these various accounts and experiences are that hard work is essential, you need to be prepared for anything, it is impossible to predict how things will turn out, and an enormous accumulated hangover is inevitable.

Other festivals

There have never before been so many festivals in Europe, ranging from the massive events at Glastonbury to the smaller, more organic local festivals in England's West Country. During the festival season the railway stations are full of expectant punters, either laden with beer and rucksacks on the way there or grimy and undefeated on the way back. The majority of festivals, in trying to give the punters as wide an experience as possible, usually feature a comedy or cabaret tent.

There is always room for comedians if you get in on the act quickly enough. You need to get your CV to the organisers shortly after the festival season is over so that they have time to get out of rehab and back into the office. As with any other gig, do not aim too high. Choose somewhere small where you can meet their standards. Festivals take place in big cities and in cowsheds around the planet, so pick carefully. Start at the festivals nearest home so you don't end up forking out for an expensive train ticket, as you often won't get paid. Comedy tents tend to run throughout most of the day at the big places, and in the evenings at the smaller ones, and as most festivals run for three to four days, that is a lot of slots to fill. The sooner you get in touch, the sooner you get on the bill.

They will give you get a free ticket, perhaps a couple, and a chance to perform, and most organisers are happy to let performers stick around and enjoy all the other goodies on site. The best-organised ones will give you a spot in the performers' field to camp, and access to at least one free meal.

Meeting other people, especially comedians, is one of the most interesting parts of performing at festivals. You never know whom you will bump into and what you will see, so keep your eyes open for the unexpected. One thing, though: although the vast majority of visitors to festivals are very supportive, doing stand-up in a hot tent to a bunch of festival-goers in various states of inebriation can be a wee bit unpredictable. Folk walk in and out of the sight lines, usually by accident rather than maliciously. As with open spots, they are not necessarily there to watch stand-up and so will not observe the usual comedy-club rules. This can be either a challenge or a lot of fun. Try it at least once – what have you got to lose? Make sure you get into festival mode rather than 'overtly professional mode'. And if you are going to get whacked out, do it after the gig. You do want to be invited back, after all. Don't you?

Starting your own comedy night

Although starting your own comedy night sounds like a daunting task it is not all that difficult: it just takes a bit of hard work, some patience and an empty venue. At this stage of your career you will clearly be looking to perform as often as possible, and if you organise a comedy night, there is no reason why you should not perform there, even if it is only a couple of minutes each time you run it.

The venue

Find a place that usually organises gigs and see when they have a vacant night. You need a separate room and a mic and PA system. If it is a regular performance space, they will have these. The actual room is important. It needs to be separate from the main bar so it feels like an entity in its own right and so you can control your environment. And it needs to have a single entrance so people do not wander in and out or just sit there talking as if in the main bar. If it is just a stage in the corner of a bar, you will be intruding on the turf of regular drinkers who will probably not want to listen to you. You need people who are there for the single purpose of watching comedy – anyone who is not carries the risk of being annoying. If there is no admission charge, then people who are merely curious and want to see what is going on can walk in and distract the comedians. Charge something, even if only a small sum, as it will inhibit the wanderers and the distracters. This means that the people who come in will want to see the gig. If it has its own bar then that's grand, but if it doesn't, then make sure people are not walking in front of the stage distracting the comedian in order to go out and get a beer. The ideal situation is an oblong room, stage at one end, door and bar at the other.

The comedy audience needs to be seated and arranged to maximise the sight lines. Organise your space. Arrange seating and tables at the front of the stage so the comedians can perform to the first few rows. Do not leave a large empty space at the front. If people don't sit at the front, then move them down or as people come in seat them so it fills up from the front. A comedian speaking to an empty space becomes disincentivised. Comedy is all about communicating and sharing jokes, so a diffused bunch of random individuals will not feel like an audience and the comedian will not feel their community.

In *Getting the Joke*, Oliver Double writes about a comedy night he organised, and how rearranging the seating made the sight lines and ambience of an awkward room more conducive to comedy: '[We] rearranged the tables . . . putting as many of the tables and chairs as close to the front as possible . . . This made it easier for an exchange of energy to occur.'[2]

Although this sounds simplistic, it makes a lot of difference. It is your gig, so make it comfortable for you as well. Steve Martin, in his book *Born Standing Up: A Comic's Life* tells of his own, unique way of dealing with a bad sight line. He decided 'to take the audience outside into the street and roam around in front of the club making wisecracks'.[3] After attempting to

hitchhike from the scene, he then flagged a taxi down and drove off, going round the block past the audience, again waving.

Filling the bill

Do not try to do it more than once a week as it will take up too much time, cause anxiety and not last the distance. Once a month is ideal, and soon people will get used to dropping in at a regular time. It is often hard to fill the bill and you may find that acts back out at the last minute, so make sure it is finalised a week or so before the gig and all the comedians have confirmed. By all means give people stage time, but do not hold a night where you cannot fill the bill and have to use comedians who did the same material two weeks ago. If you find difficulty with the bill, think about whether this should be a monthly or even less frequent gig. Do not disappoint the audience by giving the same thing week in, week out, as they will stop coming. Be adventurous and see what happens.

Decide what your position is: are you the MC, an act or just doing the promotion? It requires dedication, a fair amount of energy and goodwill, along with a few decent acts. If the competition in the town is fairly minimal, you may want to think about getting established circuit comedians on. You need to guarantee that you can pay them and that enough punters will show. However, this is stage two. Run open-mic and regular slots of unknowns first and then expand when you are established. If there is a university nearby, so much the better – these can supply audiences as well as performers.

Publicity and professionalism

Publicity is very important. If you do not publicise, then people will not come. You can advertise it as an open-mic spot but make sure you also have a few people who will definitely perform, just in case no one turns up. Appeal to folks in the area to come and support it, as it is in their interest. Use social-network sites, flyers and word of mouth to get people interested in it. Do not let the comedy night descend into an indulgent 'mates-only' night. When you are confident that it will be a good night, ring the local paper and see if they will come down and do a small piece on it. Also get the other comedians to help out with advertising. They are in a similar position to you and they have as much to gain.

The advantage of starting your own comedy night is that you are in control of the bill and the feel of the club, and you can perform there in a friendly environment. Of course, there is all that publicity stuff, money hassle and organising the acts, but it is one way of getting stage time. As long as the audience know what level of professionalism to expect, it should go fine, especially if there is a dearth of comedy venues in the area. The important thing is to be in control: of the acts, the audience and the ambience. But bear in mind that many comedy nights have only a limited longevity and a lot of nights fold after a certain time. There tends to be an exponential decrease in audience numbers unless the organisers bring in new acts or more established comedians, or offer something unique to the place.

We asked Laughing Horse what advice they had on running your own venue:

Only run a comedy night if that is what you really want to do. There's so much involved in making a night successful for audiences, venues and acts – the set-up, booking, atmosphere, promotion, staging, mechanics of running the show – that you do have to have a passion for wanting to run a comedy show, and not just want to run a gig to get more stage time (if you are a performer) or think it's a way to make a quick buck (it isn't if you run a gig properly, but can be profitable in the longer term).

When it's your own comedy night

To summarise, here's what you need to remember if you are planning to start your own comedy night:

- Most venue managers will give you a free night midweek as it boosts their bar takings on an otherwise quiet night. If you do a night at the weekend, there is more competition with other forms of entertainment.
- If it is a suitable space where other live events go on, there should be an adequate PA and lighting system, so your main focus is on the acts and publicity. It is up to you to make it happen.
- Make sure the venue is enclosed, to prevent people intruding who are not there to see comedy. And ensure there is just one entrance, to control the people coming in and out.
- Be careful whom you allow in: exclude anyone who is too drunk.
- Be sure you can fill the bill.
- Hold the gig on a regular day, even if it is only monthly or every two months.
- The best thing to hope for is to break even. If you make some cash, even better.

Comedy around the world

The comedy industry is global and there are places to perform all over the world if you look hard enough and make the effort. If you're going on holiday, why not see if there is a gig there. Obviously, if the local language is not the same as yours, this may inhibit the reception of the act slightly, but you never know. Following are a few examples from around the world.

Australia

Laughing Horse began setting up gigs at the Adelaide Fringe Festival in 2011. They have this to say about it:

It is by far the friendliest of the world's fringe festivals and is amazingly supportive of performers and shows. The Adelaidians are the most up-for-it audience in the world – there is a hunger to see visiting performers, and it's a great atmosphere. The festival is still small enough not to be overwhelming for new comedians and has a generous informality, the perfect fringe festival with the added bonus of guaranteed sunshine for three weeks!

Although there is obviously a financial consideration, Laughing Horse say it is not that much different than Edinburgh and is certainly as interesting: 'The risks are actually a lot less in packing up for a couple of months and doing the Adelaide Fringe and also the Melbourne Comedy Festival.' If you are planning a trip down under anyway, it may be worthwhile arranging your visit to coincide with both of these festivals.

Berlin

Writer and comedian James Harris has been performing stand-up in Berlin for several years now. He is also a translator and performs in both English and German. He says that the live comedy scene in Berlin is a mix of cabaret, music and clowning, and it is only recently that stand-up has become established. This is proved by Berlin stand-up Mario Barth, who performed the biggest stand-up gig in history to 70,000 spectators at the Berlin Olympiastadion in 2008. James says that there is a small English-language stand-up scene featuring comedians from all over the world. (The German scene is basically the Berlin scene, with comedians moving through the country with their shows, but in general is quite similar to London, though much smaller and with less pressure as regards time and quality.)

James says that almost all the expatriate comedians exploit their bilingualism, throwing in several German words and gaining a recognition laugh, and he goes on to say, 'It's also the case that German-language comedians are performing in English in Berlin – for instance, Otto Kuhnle, who works the UK circuit with Henning Wehn.' Knowing more than one language is a tremendous comedic resource. However, says James, 'it is also a limitation, and comedians such as Drew Portnoy and myself, who have performed in German for German audiences, would never claim that we were as funny in our adopted language.'

It is possible to do stand-up just in English at certain venues and there are also English-only nights in Cologne and Munich. However, comedians should remember that it is helpful to make reference to German culture in order to build a relationship with the audience: 'Stand-ups who make no cultural concessions to their audience seem to me to be on a hiding to nothing,' says James. He thinks Germany is a great place to get gig practice on the cheap. The best thing is to be in touch with the organisers of the SIN club or with Summer Banks at Comedy Gone Wild, Berlin's longest-running English-language open mic.

When initially asked about performing live comedy in Berlin, the comedian Rey Melara suggested that 'doing English language comedy in Berlin is like selling suntan lotion to Eskimos. They wouldn't really know what to do with it.' In a slightly more positive mode, Rey feels that although there is an English-speaking presence on the German comedy circuit, it is growing slowly and the abilities of the comedians are varied. But, he says, 'I have seen talent here, no doubt about it.' Although the audiences include native Germans, 'expats are a big part of what we do'. Rey's advice to anyone going to Berlin and trying stand-up is 'to do their best stuff, have a beer after the show with fellow comedians and audience members that stick around, and just enjoy it. It is great to try new things and meet interesting people. That's what I get out of it. It's just a matter of doing something with it with a positive outcome.' Like any comedy circuit anywhere, comedians need to be aware of their uniqueness and what sets them apart from the comedians on before and after them. According to Rey, in Berlin, by definition, English-speaking comedy 'does fill some need for a different kind of comedy'.

Comedian David Deery, who moved from Brooklyn, New York, to live and perform in Berlin, says that the Germans 'have a weird sense of humour, and by weird I obviously mean non-existent'. On a more practical note, he recommends that comedians trying out material in Berlin need to 'write some good jokes and get out there, let your shit fly and hope none of it, or beer bottles, get thrown back in your face. In reality, slapstick and music always transcends culture. Everyone laughs at a guy getting kicked in the balls, even Germans.' He says his own act is 'based on me being me and not based on any language (although I speak English)'. If your act involves some musical or physical aspect it would be better to focus on that rather than puns that may go straight over the audience's heads. Watch how other comedians deal with the language barrier before you go, and adjust your set to suit.

Jerusalem

The Off The Wall comedy club has been running in Jerusalem for several years now and gets comedians dropping in from all over the globe. David Kilimnick, an American migrant to Israel, says that in general it's becoming a lively scene:

There is a growing grassroots scene developing. We, the Off The Wall Comedy Basement, are the first comedy club in Jerusalem. Since we opened, the comedy form of expression has become a popular outlet for people in the city. The Jerusalem style of comedy is starting to gain popularity. Comedians joke about life in Israel as there are a lot of cultural differences and the clashing worlds make for good comedy. The Israeli comedians talk about family and grade school. I focus on single life, emigrating to a new country, family, religion and anything I feel in my heart. Religion makes its way into everybody's routine at some point.

The audiences are varied, as the city's community is quite mixed and there are a lot of visitors. Israelis and immigrants go to see specific shows in Hebrew while the shows in English get lots of tourists and immigrants as well as locals. David says that 'the Arabic-speaking audience in our area is good with Hebrew and English too'.

Many established comedians, as well as amateurs from other countries like America, Australia and the UK, perform at the club, although the place is too small for the really big names. Off The Wall offers any visiting comedians a very interesting place to perform. As usual, visiting comedians do best when they offer their opinions about where they are before doing their regular routines.

Obviously, subject matter must be a major consideration here, and tact is needed where political and religious issues are concerned. David says:

Religion is the one thing that you have to be careful with. You have to also watch out for politics, as everybody is a political debater in Israel. Basically, like any country, you have to not go over that line of hurt. Since there are many cultures, jokes about different cultures and races are a big topic. Even so, if it falls under 'racist' in mixed community shows, nobody will laugh.

Hecklers are not a significant factor in comedy nights in Jerusalem. David is not keen on their interruptions: 'Hecklers always suck. The heckler comes there with hate, and all you want is love. Because love is what brings laughs. That is what we are going for in Jerusalem. At least *I* am going for that.'

Teaching comedy

Ed Aczel did it at night after work, Jimmy Carr and Shazia Mirza both did it when they were starting off, and many more have been to classes run by comedians in order to improve their material and the way they perform it. When we are starting out we need as much advice as possible if we are to avoid all the horrendous mistakes a lot of other people have made in our positions. It is amazing how a short conversation with an experienced performer can save a lot of heartache in the future. Performing live comedy is tough and rejection is unpleasant, but there are people and organisations who can help comedians with their acts when they are starting out.

When I started the degree course at Solent University in Southampton, there was a mini-media flurry, the negative side of which focused on the idea that 'you can't teach funny', which we agree with. What the degree does is tutor those people who already have an innate ability to make an audience laugh. We help them refine their craft through positive feedback and having the opportunity to try out material in a supportive environment. There are other universities and colleges in the UK and the US who do similar courses. There is also a university in Humber, Canada, that runs a diploma course featuring stand-up, writing, improv and physical comedy as well as the business of comedy.

With a little research it is possible to find a place that suits you. Ed Aczel first went to the Amused Moose comedy course

in London when he was starting out: 'I didn't really have any interest in performing originally. I needed something to do in the evening because I was bored at work so I did the course at the Amused Moose and started doing stand-up.'

The Comedy School in London runs courses for young comedians, and its annual Funny Festival is as entertaining as it is informative. The school also does outreach work in local communities to help people find their creative voice and engage with a possible career they may not have thought about before. Keith Palmer is director of the Comedy School, which is situated in a beautiful building next to Regent's Park. Usually busy with comedians, students and other interested parties, it is a great place to spend time absorbing as much information about the comedy industry as possible.

The stand-up comedian Ivor Dembina runs a workshop for beginner stand-ups at the Funny Festival. He believes that the key to engaging an audience is for a comedian to be interesting to them. One of his exercises is to get the performer to 'think of something true and talk about it for a minute without being boring'. Dembina then asks the other participants what the interesting points were. He stresses that the persona of the comedian is also the vehicle of the comedy: in an age of gossip and celebrity-hood 'putting the me in it' is the selling point. People *do* want to know about the lives of others, but it is how interesting that life sounds that transforms it into a marketable commodity – which takes us back to the importance of branding. For Dembina, the material involves you rather than other people, so personalisation is essential. He says that comedy can be either vicarious or can involve mutual experience: we either listen to people talking about something that we haven't done ourselves or we connect with the comedian because we have shared events in our lives.

Dembina believes that comedians should explore personal dislikes, too – the self-loathing or shared prejudices they have that make a connection with the audience. When demonstrating a heckling exercise, he stresses that most heckling is not threatening but inclusive, and the comedian should therefore respond naturally. Prepared comebacks can be too savage and lose the spontaneity of the moment. As he says, 'Trust yourself, you are funny.'

The comedian Arnold Brown points out that there is a difference between the world 'as it is' and the world 'as I see it'. How the media represents the world and how each comedian sees the world are very different, and this gives comedians a unique angle that we should amplify in order to give our comedy a unique flavour. The problem with the comedy market is one of homogeneity: too many comedians have similar backgrounds, which leads to similar material. The more different we are, the better we become.

The American Comedy Institute (ACI) in New York is organised by Stephen Rosenfeld, who says it 'was started by comedians who wanted to work with me on their writing and their performing skills and wanted me to see their work in the clubs, to give them feedback and help them improve'. According to Stephen, 'comedians come to ACI from all over the world' and his main advice for people coming to the States to perform is to 'avoid local UK jokes. Focus on universal material – relationships, family, things we have in common. Also, American audiences enjoy seeing the US through your eyes' so a bit of observational or topical material will go down well. Tell them what you think of the States or New York in particular and compare it with home – American audiences, like comedy audiences elsewhere, value insights into how others see their country.

According to Stephen, American comedians joke about 'their feelings about what's going on in their lives, and their feelings about what's going on around them – politically, culturally, socially, etc.' There are, as anywhere, certain subjects that American audiences will not be too happy about comedians commenting on: 'It's not good to joke about tragedies that just happened.' Stephen confirms that heckling is not common in New York: 'There are fewer hecklers here than in UK. Most shows don't have hecklers.' Which is probably a welcome relief.

The teachers: Oliver Double

Oliver Double was one of the first people to establish live comedy in an academic context. While working as a comedian he completed his PhD on stand-up at Sheffield University and is now teaching at Kent University. Olly says that because you cannot teach people to be funny and they have to already have the innate ability to make people laugh, the job of the comedy teacher is to identify and nurture the students' natural talent.

The teacher must also beware of imposing standards or styles on the students, as they need to see what they can be capable of in order to develop their unique comic voice. It is this individuality that needs to be encouraged, he says: 'When you see students doing something interesting, unique, bizarre, or just different from the run of the mill, encourage them to try it onstage. If they do and it works, encourage them to see how much further they can take it. Unless you understand the people you're teaching as individuals, you might as well give up.'

Stage time is essential: the more the better. Olly's students do their first gig after ten days of starting the course, as the only place to really learn is in a live context. They then, in each successive week, have to develop more material to be performed live. Comedy always involves the risk of failing to be funny, so a supportive and informal atmosphere is required: 'The more the students think they're not really working, the more creative they become. Messing about can be very productive for putting together a stand-up act.' He has faced a degree of scepticism from the media, which does not always understand what the classes actually consist of or the value of comedy as a communicative and performable medium. And comedians have been just as bad:

There's an awful lot of mystique that surrounds stand-up comedians. If you buy into the idea that comic talent is an inborn gift, which expresses itself unproblematically from the first moment the comedian steps onstage, then the idea of teaching stand-up is totally pointless. However, in reality all comedians *learn* how to do stand-up. No matter how talented, they start off by being bad (or at least highly inconsistent), and by an often-painful process of trial-and-error gain enough experience to be able to express their talent.

The teachers: Jill Edwards

Jill Edwards is the UK's leading stand-up comedy coach, whose workshops at the Komedia in Brighton aim to 'demystify the art of stand-up comedy' and help performers find their 'inner comic'. Jill performed as a stand-up comedian as well as one half of the comedy duo Pep Talk. She created the first stand-up course at City Lit in Holborn, London, and she has worked with, among many others, Jimmy Carr and Shazia Mirza. As Jimmy Carr says, 'People say comedy can't be taught. They could learn a lot from Jill Edwards.'

Jill recognised a gap in the market and realised the potential usefulness of a course teaching people the rudiments of stand-up, not only on how to perform but also how to get work on the circuit. Initially, people were sceptical but then Malcolm Hay, the respected comedy reviewer from London magazine *Time Out*, wrote a good review which validated her work.

After interviewing comedians' bookers on what they thought comedians ought to know, Jill decided that, rather than teach people how *she* would perform live comedy, she should train them in what they could do naturally but better. As she says, 'Training in a profession you want to go into is always useful.' She focused on finding their unique voices, as she believes that 'everyone has an inner comic: if you can laugh, you have a sense of humour; if you have a sense of humour, you have an inner comic. And everyone's inner comic is different.'

One of the main things Jill helps comedians with is structuring their act so it works to maximum effect. This includes how to start and how to build the set to a conclusion. She explains, 'Agents know when it's not right. All professional comics have very good structure.' She also emphasises that comedians should not waste time with their material and should be as economical as possible:

The set-up must be as short as possible to get to the punchline as quickly as you can. In a gag, the set-up is in the real world which the audience is in, and the punchline is from the comic's world. Every time the punchline is from your world, you're constantly creating a connection with the audience in telling them how you see the world. The intention isn't just to make you laugh but to communicate with you. What I teach the students is don't go on desperate for laughs – communicate.

Jill feels that her classes empower people to do this and give them plenty of time to experiment, trying things out. She shows people how to deal with hecklers and dying at gigs, as well as how to get work on the circuit and the practicalities of the business side of comedy. At the end of the course the students get to do the act they have developed in front of an invited audience. And from there on, they are on their own.

Recap

In this chapter you have had an insight into how comedy works and how you can best position yourself in it. You need to decide what style of comedy you are going to do and who the likely audience is going to be, and your publicity material should give new punters an idea as to what kind of material you are going to do. Maintaining a web presence is free, and keeping a regular blog or updating your webpage with new information is essential.

You can keep your diary filled by always asking to return at a later date but you must have new material, and it is this incentive that can keep comedians writing regularly. Do not be lazy. Not only can you do gigs at other venues but you can set up your own. There are things to watch out for but there is no harm in giving it a go.

There are more festivals now than ever before, and these can also be new and interesting places to perform at. And not just domestic ones: live comedy is performed in many other countries and it is not difficult to combine a holiday with a bit of extra work. Performing in other countries presents new challenges but they are in no way insurmountable, and local audiences will be pleased that you have made the effort. Commenting on the country or city where you are performing is a good way to build a relationship with the audience.

You can always do better, no matter how many gigs you do, and there are teachers around who can guide you in short courses and even degree courses. Building up your career is an interesting challenge and it is up to you to make the most of it.

10. Round-up

Performing live comedy is not an impossible dream, we merely have to apply ourselves and put a lot of effort into it. We have seen that the comedy circuit is an open one and we just have to get our first gig in order to launch our careers. It's that simple. This book has covered a lot of important aspects of the process, but there is no substitute for getting out there and doing it. We have looked at the reasons why people do it and one of the main ones is that we feel we have something to say. We have comic aptitude and the ability to make others laugh so can therefore structure our ideas into comedy.

But we also need to think about how to perform it: our stage identities need careful consideration, as even the smallest of details can make a difference as to how the audience perceives us. Building a relationship with the audience is crucial. If they do not feel anything towards us or are bored by us, the gig is up. We have choices about how to present ourselves onstage – either 'heightened' so we can talk from our own personal perspective and experiences, or through comic characters that we have developed, so we can talk from other points of view. Live comedy is not just about delivering a string of gags but can involve lots of different approaches, with props, magic, music and ventriloquism. And we do not have to be up there on our own to do it – we can always work with a partner in a double act or a small comedy group.

This book has shown you ways of avoiding the pitfalls that new comedians come across – a bit of sound advice can save a lot of trouble in the future. We can prepare ourselves for any eventuality but we must also know that we have the comic skills to deal with anything that may occur while we are up there.

Audiences do not just go to comedy to look at us; they come to listen as well. Hopefully the tried and tested exercises in this book have been helpful and have opened up other possibilities that you hadn't thought of. For material, look closer to home, at yourself and the things around you, so you can always be truthful. Jokes are important but so are aptitude and confidence – if we do not appear confident, then the audience will not trust us and, again, the gig is up. We have to trust our audience and find a way of reaching out to them, of finding common ground so they can relate to what we are talking about and find it as funny as we do.

The comedy industry is global and there is no need for us to stay local. Look abroad, at festivals, and at the possibility of moving beyond performing live comedy and into areas like radio and television. If we have something worth talking about, and have the confidence and skills to make good comedy, then we simply need to find the right audience. Finally, I hope you follow the advice in this book, as I have spent nearly thirty years thinking about live comedy and how it works, and most of my advice is pretty sound. If not, get in touch. And good luck.

Bibliography

Allen, Tony, *A Summer in the Park: A Journal of Speakers' Corner*, London: Freedom Press, 2004

Allen, Tony, *Attitude: The Secret of Stand-Up Comedy*, Glastonbury: Gothic Image Publications, 2002

Bruce, Lenny: *The Almost Unpublished Lenny Bruce*, Philadelphia: Running Press, 1984

Bruce, Lenny, *How to Talk Dirty and Influence People: An Autobiography*, St. Albans: Panther, 1975

Carr, Jimmy, and Lucy Greeves, *The Naked Jape: Uncovering the Hidden World of Jokes*, London: Penguin, 2006

Cohen, John, *The Essential Lenny Bruce: His Original Unexpurgated Satirical Routines*, St Albans: Panther, 1975

Cook, William, *Ha Bloody Ha: Comedians Talking*, London: Fourth Estate, 1994

Double, Oliver, *Getting the Joke: The Art of Stand-Up Comedy*, London: Methuen Drama, 2005

Double, Oliver, *Stand-Up! On Being a Comedian*, London: Methuen Drama, 1997

Fisher, Mark, *The Edinburgh Fringe Survival Guide: How to Make Your Show a Success*, London: Methuen Drama, 2012

Goldman, Albert, *Ladies and Gentlemen, Lenny Bruce*, New York: Random House, 1974

Hall, Julian, *The Rough Guide to Cult Comedy*, London: Rough Guides, 2006

Hardee, Malcolm, and John Fleming, *I Stole Freddie Mercury's Birthday Cake*, London: Fourth Estate, 1996

Long, Rob, *Conversations with My Agent*, London: Faber & Faber, 1996

Martin, Steve, *Born Standing Up: A Comic's Life*, London: Pocket Books, 2008

Skinner, Frank, *Frank Skinner*, London: Century, 2001

Wilmut, Roger, and Peter Rosengard, *Didn't You Kill My Mother-in-Law? The Story of Alternative Comedy in Britain from the Comedy Store to Saturday Live*, London: Methuen Drama, 1989

Notes

CHAPTER 1

1 The radical American
intellectual Noam Chomsky

CHAPTER 3

1 Double, *Stand-Up!*, p. 243
2 Allen, *Attitude: The Secret of
Stand-Up Comedy*, p. 36
3 Wilmut and Rosengard, *Didn't
You Kill My Mother-in-Law?*,
p. 49
4 Cook, *Ha Bloody Ha*, p. 74
5 *Comedy Studies Journal*, 1.1
6 *Comedy Studies Journal*, 1.2
7 Cook, *op. cit.*, p. 71

CHAPTER 6

1 Skinner, *Frank Skinner*, p. 319
2 Cook, *Ha Bloody Ha*, p. 126–7
3 Double, *Getting the Joke*, p. 190
4 Martin, *Born Standing Up*, p. 1
5 Cohen, *The Essential Lenny
Bruce*, p. 140

CHAPTER 7

1 Bruce, *How to Talk Dirty and
Influence People*, p. 41
2 Double, *Getting the Joke*, p. 206
3 Cohen, *The Essential Lenny
Bruce*, p. 138
4 Ed Byrne, *Pedantic & Whimsical*
DVD, 2006
5 Skinner, *Frank Skinner*, p. 266
6 Long, *Conversations with My
Agent*, p. 69
7 Skinner, *op. cit.*, p. 300

8 Martin, *Born Standing Up*,
p. 72–3
9 Skinner, *op. cit.*, p. 301

CHAPTER 8

1 Cohen, *The Essential Lenny
Bruce*, p. 199
2 Double, *Stand-Up!*, p. 24–5
3 Hardee and Fleming, *I Stole
Freddie Mercury's Birthday
Cake*, p. 150
4 Cook, *Ha Bloody Ha*, p. 199
5 *Ibid.*, p. 206
6 Skinner, *Frank Skinner*, p. 319
7 Cook, *op. cit.*, p. 217
8 Allen, *A Summer in the Park*,
p. 93
9 Cook, *op. cit.*, p. 124
10 *Ibid*, p. 126
11 Bruce, *op. cit.*, p. 192
12 Cook, *op. cit.*, p. 218
13 *Ibid.*, p. 247
14 Allen, *op. cit.*, p. 38
15 Double, *op. cit.*, p. 134
16 Double, *Getting the Joke*, p. 194
17 *Ibid.*, p. 195
18 Cook, *op. cit.*, p. 222
19 Skinner, *op. cit.*, p. 16
20 Cook, *op. cit.*, p. 222
21 *Ibid.*, p. 229

CHAPTER 9

1 Fisher, *The Edinburgh Fringe
Survival Guide*, p. 79–80
2 Double, *Getting the Joke*, p. 110
3 Martin, *Born Standing Up*, p. 148

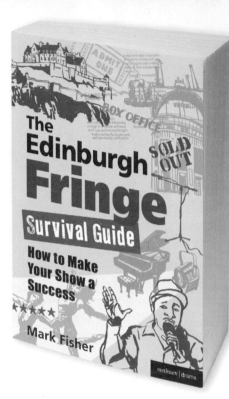